BATIK

modern concepts and techniques

BATIK

modern concepts and techniques

NOEL DYRENFORTH

Batsford

First published 2003

Text © Noel Dyrenforth 2003

Volume © B T Batsford

The right of Noel Dyrenforth to be identified as Author of this work has been asserted to him in accordance with the Copyright, Designs and Patents Act 1988.

Photography by Michael Wicks

ISBN 07134 8778 X

A CIP catalogue record for this book is available from the British Library.

Printed in Singapore by Kyodo Printing Co.

for the publishers

B T Batsford
64 Brewery Road
London N7 9NY
England
www.batsford.com

A member of Chrysalis Books plc

CONTENTS

Opposite: canting; *Flex* Noel Dyrenforth; application of dye.

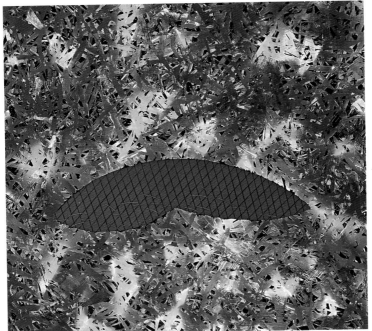

FOREWORD

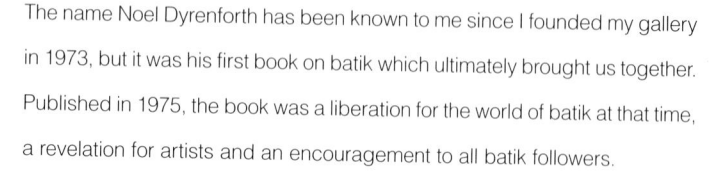

The name Noel Dyrenforth has been known to me since I founded my gallery in 1973, but it was his first book on batik which ultimately brought us together. Published in 1975, the book was a liberation for the world of batik at that time, a revelation for artists and an encouragement to all batik followers.

In my Cologne gallery, I had specialized entirely in works by Indonesian batik artists and had ended up in a rut. Further artistic development was no longer discernible. Noel Dyrenforth's book opened up a new horizon for me. I liked his style, his educational approach and the ideas that he was able to translate into batik. I gathered all my courage and wrote to him in London asking for an appointment.

How relieved I was to discover that he was not the lofty practitioner I expected to meet, but rather the good friend from next door. From the outset he created an inspirational and unrestrained atmosphere which made a great friendship possible. His renowned English sense of humour, appreciated world-wide, has also contributed to our 25-year long association.

Noel Dyrenforth's assured taste and style, as well as his close ties with batik artists throughout Europe, left me in his wake. However, I was able to make a small contribution. I had learned about the art of batik in Java, where Yogyakarta was Indonesia's prime cultural centre in the early 1970s. On my extended travels I had made friends with such eminent batik artists as Amri Yahya, Bambang Oetoro and Ardiyanto, among others. I saw the rapid changes which were taking place year after year

in Java and advised Noel to visit the 'promised land' of batik, sooner rather than later. The living museum was almost coming to an end but it enabled Noel to experience the full splendour of Yogyakarta in its prime.

If anyone today can write a book on the subject of batik, it is Noel Dyrenforth. He has the contacts with artists world-wide, and he has the necessary perseverance and years of experience. He has a sure taste and makes very high artistic demands both on himself and on his chosen colleagues.

Noel does not think English, nor European, but global – a messenger of batik with a world view. He seeks to motivate and inspire, and in doing so, not only sets new trends, but also a new benchmark. In this book he brings together internationally recognized batik artists to present the reader with a work that is written from the heart and which testifies to his connoisseurship and personal engagement in the subject of batik art.

Rudolf G. Smend

ACKNOWLEDGEMENTS

I am deeply grateful for all the support I have received in writing this book. My appreciation is boundless as my work is woven into my daily life. Batik has made me many friends, from the man in Java who makes the cantings to the curator of the Victoria and Albert Museum. Teaching has been a mission; students and artists alike have played a constructive part in my attitude to creativity. Batik has also linked me with other cultures, particularly in my travels. It has enriched as well as reaffirmed my faith in humanity and coexistence.

My special thanks go to Christa Corner whose struggles with my handwriting never distracted her from making valuable contributions while processing the text very efficiently – and not without a few laughs. To Michael Wicks, who spent days patiently photographing all the techniques from every conceivable angle, with excellent results. To Rudolf and Karen Smend who took the initiative in 1973 and opened a Textile Art Gallery promoting excellence and innovation. Their friendship and support for my work is unequivocal. To Tina Persaud, managing editor at Batsford, whose enthusiasm for the book was very persuasive and a great incentive. Finally, my thanks to all the artists featured in the book. They have been an inspiration to me.

INTRODUCTION

As part of the emerging counter-culture of the early 1960s, I was eagerly seeking an alternative to the conventional art processes. I found it in batik. Painting hot wax and liquid colour on to cloth seemed a volatile and radical mix, in keeping with the mode of the times.

Batik had little or no artistic legacy in the West, which liberated me from the constraints of content, style and practice. Equally, I found in batik a means to resolve the historic dichotomy of art versus craft.

Since those heady days of discovery, my passion has continued to infuse my creativity. The spirit of the work is underpinned by the discipline of the essential technique. Integrity and sensibilities are constantly being reappraised to enrich the expression.

I have attempted to interpret my experience and innovations by graphically detailing the step-by-step processes. The projects are devised to exploit the unique nature of the wax-resist technique, while stimulating creative potential. Both modern and traditional methods are included. Dyeing is extensively covered with brush, dip, spray and discharge application. Waxing with brush, canting, stamp, stencil and etching on cloth, paper and wood gives the artist a wide choice of options.

The internationally renowned artists featured have all utilized the wax-resist dyed medium with conviction and sensitivity. Their concepts are undoubtedly empowered by their affinity with batik.

Besides being a practical resource, I sincerely hope that the book will inspire a wider use and appreciation of this unique visual medium.

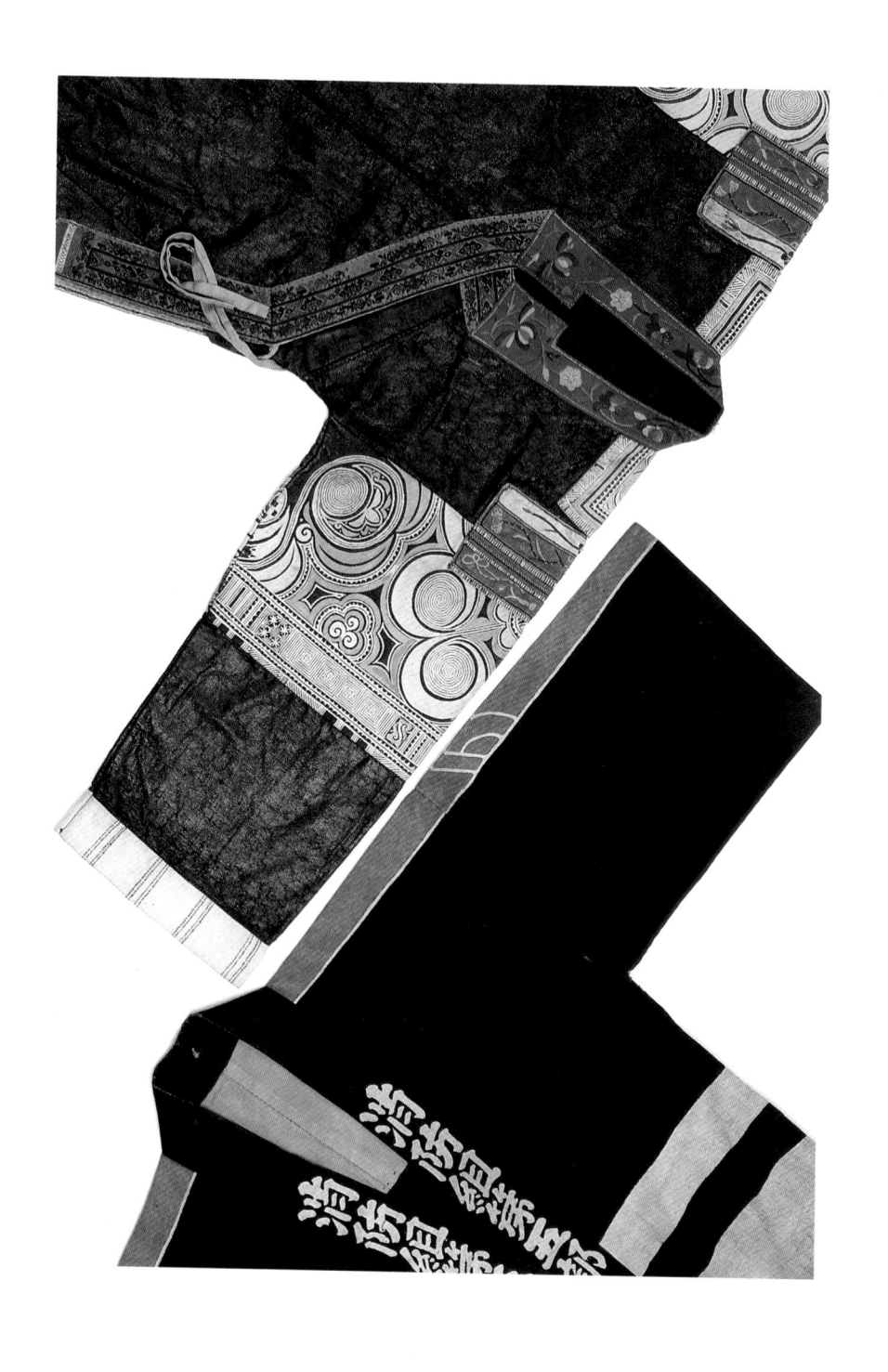

Miao costume from Guizhou Province, China. Wax-resist

dyed indigo. Japanese fireman's jacket. Paste-resiste dyed

indigo.

TRADITION AND DEVELOPMENT

The word *batik* is of Javanese origin. The word *ambatik*, derived from *tik*, means to mark with spots or dots and, in a wider sense, signifies drawing, painting or writing. No such word is to be found in the old Javanese language, so we must conclude that batik is a word of fairly recent origin. It is recorded for the first time in Dutch texts of the 17th century in a reference to a shipload of fabrics with coloured designs.

Batik is the word used to denote a particular method of applying coloured designs to fabric. This method involves covering certain sections of the design with a substance, usually liquid wax, so that the fabric underneath retains its original colour while the material is subjected to the action of dyes. The covering substance, whether wax, rice paste or mud, is referred to as the resist. Fabrics thus treated may be monochrome or polychrome, depending upon the number of resist applications and the number of times it is dyed.

The origins of batik are disputed by scholars. The earliest evidence has been found in five separate regions: the Far East, the Middle East, Central Asia, India and Peru. It is conceivable that these areas developed independently, without the influence of trade or cultural exchanges. However, with the exception of Peru (where an independent development must be assumed), it is more likely that the craft spread from China to the islands of the Malay Archipelago and westwards to the Middle East through the caravan routes. Of these early examples, perhaps the most important collection is that preserved in the Shōsōin Repository of Imperial Treasures in Nara, Japan, which dates from the eighth century.

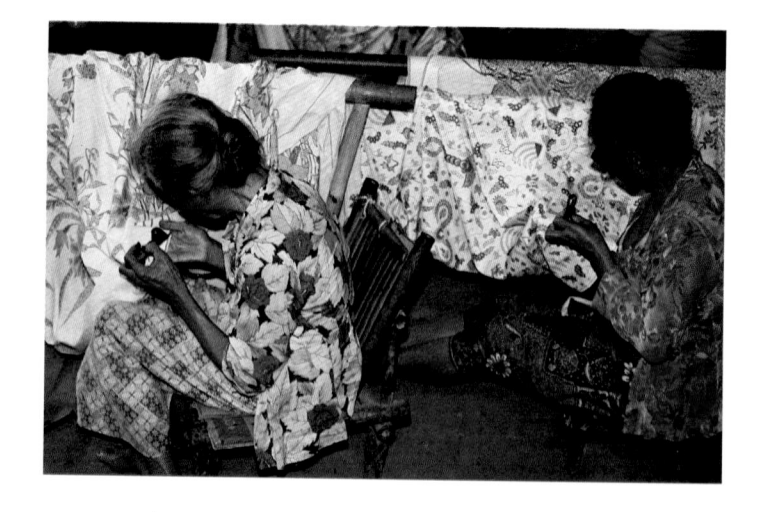

Certainly, batik was practised in China as early as the Western Han

dynasty (202–8 BC) and it is highly probably that silk batiks were exported to Japan, to Central Asia and, via the silk route, to the Middle East and India. In India, the technique was transferred to cotton. No evidence of batiks prior to the 16th century has yet been discovered in India, probably because the climate is not conducive to the conservation of fabrics. However, seventh century frescos in the Ajanta caves depict head-wraps and garments which could well have been batiks. Similarly, temple ruins in Java and Bali dating back to the 13th century contain figures whose garments are patterned in a manner suggestive of batik. By 1677, there is evidence that a considerable Chinese export trade to Java, Sumatra, Persia and Hindustan was in progress. Excavations conducted by Sir Aurel Stein in the Central Asian steppes of Xinjiang and Gansu provinces yielded examples of batik. Most of these were of silk, but one, decorated with blue and white motifs in cotton, has been identified as Indian. The silk cloths appear to originate from China and are probably of the Tang dynasty (AD 618–907).

In Egypt, linen, and occasionally woollen fabrics, have been excavated, bearing white patterns on a blue ground. Although they have been used as shrouds, there is reason to believe that they originally served as hangings or altar covers in churches. These batiks were made in Egypt and possibly also in Syria and date from the fifth century AD.

Indonesia, however – and most particularly the island of Java – is the area where batik has reached its greatest peak of accomplishment. Initially, it was the pastime of privileged women of noble birth, but gradually it came to be the distinguishing mark of the dress of the aristocracy, and as its popularity increased, servants of aristocratic households and members of other sections of society were gradually involved in batik production. Finally, it came to be a national costume worn all over the islands.

Batik was introduced into Holland in the 17th century with the colonization of Java by the Dutch. At the time, the designs were too exotic for popular taste. This perception was changed two centuries later when the British temporarily colonized Java (1811–1816) and the then Lieutenant Governor, Sir Thomas Stamford Raffles, published a history of batik. This aroused a great deal of interest and led to an intense study of the market potential of batik-printed cloth, the methods and dyes employed in making it, and the possibility of developing machinery to produce imitations of batik prints that would be cheaper than hand-crafted originals.

The British found it was not an easy matter to produce batik imitations on a large scale, nor imitate the richness of the originals. It was difficult to match the local vegetable dyes and the patterns were of such complexity that an enormous number of interlocking blocks and rollers were required to reproduce them, making the cost prohibitive.

The Dutch, on the other hand, established a factory in Leiden in 1835, and very rapidly other factories followed at Rotterdam, Appledoorn, Helmond and Haarlem, where attempts were made to produce batiks using the same techniques as those employed in Indonesia. Large numbers of Indonesian artisans were brought in and established in specifically built villages for the purpose of teaching the craft to Dutch workers. These Dutch workers, in turn, practised the craft in Holland before being transferred to the East Indies where they supervised the construction of state-controlled combines, uniting individual and family workshops.

In the early 1840s, the Swiss had begun to export imitation batik sarongs, and at this point, the Javanese workshops developed a form of wax-block printing adapted from Indian techniques and known as *cap*, so that by the late 1870s the Swiss could no longer maintain the cost-effectiveness of their production.

By the early 1900s, the Germans developed *cantings* made of glass, and electrically heated wax-writing devices with button-controlled spouts for the mass production of batiks. These methods were particularly effective in producing furnishing and curtaining fabrics, some of which retained areas of wax in a limited way so that they produced attractive semi-translucent effects.

In the general economic collapse of the early 1930s the large-scale commercial production of batiks ceased. The process became once more

The Miao tribe use a fluted, triangular metal tool, similar to a calligraphy pen, to apply wax to the cloth. The clear, unbroken line is produced by using only beeswax, which is both tenacious and flexible.

An example of the refined skill of the waxing process. Undyed cotton, 22 x 16 cm (8 $^1/_2$ x 6 $^1/_4$ in), Miao tribe.

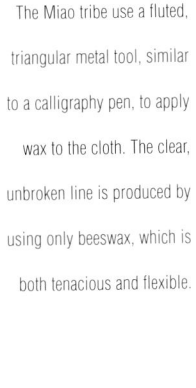

the province of individual craftsmen in the Far East, while in Europe it was developed by artist craftsmen. Museums in Haarlem were, as a result of Holland's colonization in the East, a rich source of material, and it is therefore not surprising that a school of batik design, known as the Haarlem School, developed there. By 1900 batik had become a standard feature of arts and crafts exhibitions. A fine, decorative ornamentation gained influence in Holland, integrating Javanese and Dutch traditions and contributing to the Art Nouveau style. Among the names associated with this development are Chris Lebeau, Leon Cachet, Thorn Prikker, Gerrit Dijsselhof, Colenbrander, Berta Bake and Marguerite Pangon.

The far-reaching consequences of exposure to the batik art of the East can be seen in the work of many 20th-century designers, among them Roger Fry and Charles Rennie Mackintosh. Today, batik is recognized as an art form in its own right. It also has a particular value in crossing cultural divides, embracing indigenous form and individual creativity.

AFRICA

A tradition of resist-dyeing is also part of the history of Africa. For centuries the Yoruba people of southern Nigeria and the Soninke and Wolof tribes of Senegal have practised dyeing involving the use of resist. In the case of the Yoruba, cassava paste is used, while the Soninke employ rice paste. In recent times wax products have replaced the traditional materials in some areas. The mud cloths of the Bambara people of Mali are produced by a technique similar in principle to batik.

The cloths are dipped for a day in a dye produced by boiling the bark of certain trees. Mud from ferrous ponds is then applied with a scoop to produce a pattern. When dried, an alkali soap bleaches the cloth to reveal a lighter background.

CHINA

Chinese batik has a recorded history of more than 2,000 years. Indigo-dyed batik first appeared during the Han dynasty (206 BC–AD 220). Today it still flourishes. Indigo batik is widely practised as a folk art and is mainly concentrated in south-west China in the provinces of Guizhou and Yunnan. These areas have maintained their social customs and traditions to this day, despite the influence of the predominantly Han culture.

The minority tribes of these provinces live in inaccessible mountain terrain and have developed a distinctive batik art. The principal ethnic groups are the Miao of Guizhou province and the Bai and Yi of Yunnan provinces. The girls learn the craft from their mothers. The first gift a girl will give to her prospective husband would be a batik ribbon, and her dowry is considered to be the quality of her own skill, showing how indispensable batik is as part of daily life. It is little wonder that batik has become such a highly developed skill. The patterns convey something of the joy and continuity of life. Although tourism is always a threat to standards, they are carefully monitored to preserve the integrity of the art form for future generations.

INDIA

The main centres of batik today are on the south-eastern part of the Deccan plateau and the Coromandel coast. The batik industry was at its peak in the 17th and 18th centuries when exports were made to many parts of the world, including Java, Persia and Europe. The traditional method used in the south-eastern Deccan was batik combined with colouring and painting. The pen used for waxing is called a *kalam*. It consists of a metal needle set into a bamboo handle, wrapped in about 6 cm (2¹/₂ in) of absorbent fibre or hair which acts as a reservoir for the molten wax. Pressure on the wad regulates the flow.

The work of waxing is done by men who must belong to the caste of indigo dyers. After the first waxing they prepare the cloth again for a further waxing and painting on of colour by a process of washing, beating and tanning. This latter process is considered comparatively easy and is usually completed by children.

JAPANESE ROKETSU-ZOME

The earliest evidence of wax-resist dyed cloth is preserved in the Shōsōin Repository in Nara. These date from the eighth century and were known then as Rokechi. During the Nara period (710–794, when Nara was the capital of Japan) the Chinese Tang dynasty influence was clearly identifiable in technique and design. It is possible that Japanese artisans were working under the supervision of Chinese *émigré* craftsmen. The majority of Rokechi textiles were created with wooden stamps dipped in

wax and printed on silk. Knowledge of vegetable dyes and mordants was imported from China and India. Out of an amazing 180,000 textiles and fragments collected in the Shō sō in, perhaps the best-known Rokechi pieces are the four screens used by the Emperor Shomu (reigned 724–749). Each screen measures 163 x 57 cm (64 x 23 in) and consists of designs of animals and plant life. Rōkechi declined rapidly in the subsequent Heian period (794–1185) due to isolationist policies when all imports of foreign culture were curtailed.

During the Edo period (1600–1868) Japan enjoyed a period of stability and exquisite indulgence in the arts. The essence of this refinement was reflected in the kimono. An explicit style developed to display taste and professional status more graphically than was possible in the West. Yuzen was a technique that was developed by a Kyoto fan maker of that name. It consisted of applying a fine resist line of rice paste with a cane to the cloth and filling the spaces with dye colour. Yuzen became the fashionable process of decoration and remains in the mainstream today.

Japan's reawakening of its own wax-resist legacy came around 1900. At this time the textile treasures of the Shosoin became available for study, and interest was also spurred by the introduction of batik in Europe. The principal of the Kyoto Industrial Arts Institute, Tsuruichi Tsurumaki, was credited with introducing the process as a fine-art technique. Roketsu-zome (or sometimes the shorter form Rozome) is the preferred term for the technique today. There are many artists devoted to this medium, creating and contributing individually to a body of work of high standard and winning international recognition. The distinctive feature of Roketsu-zome artists is the utilization of traditional techniques of dyeing, using shading and control to energize their work.

MACHINE WAX PRINTING

Since the mid-19th century, the Dutch had been producing an industrial wax print, imitative of the Javanese style, for the African market. By the end of that century Britain, through its colonial development, opened up further markets which the Dutch could not cater for. The African print industry was begun in Manchester by the firm Brunnschweiler, a division of Tootal. In more recent years, through a process of Africanization, a demand for native styles and designs has largely replaced European styles of dress. In Nigeria alone, which today has a population of some 117 million, a strong preference was shown for the wax print over other printed techniques. Today in Africa, works have been set up to produce wax prints which, in time, will surely rival the quality of the imports and become independent. Many such businesses have now acquired the equipment and technical skills to reproduce their own distinctive designs.

Strictly speaking, the African 'wax print' is a misnomer: the resist is, in fact, pine resin, dark brown in colour and tacky in consistency when heated. The resist patterns are printed on the cloth by two engraved copper rollers rotating together. The resin is cooled and pulled through a pot-eye to remove and marble the resin before dyeing. The cloth is passed through an indigo vat; it then oxidizes and passes over a series of creepers or racks. This combined process of dipping and oxidizing is repeated four times to get the full depth of the indigo. Other colours are added after the cloth is washed and dried and treated with naphthol; the cloth is then passed through a bath of an azo dye, whereupon coupling (chemical bonding) takes place and the colour develops. Finally, the cloth is cleaned of resin, washed and finished.

EUROPE

During the second half of the 19th century, European interests in the Oriental arts coincided with the movement to revive handicrafts. In Britain, John Ruskin and William Morris, concerned about the rapid growth in mechanization, inspired a re-evaluation of society's attitude to work and its social implications. They proposed that the divisions between Arts and Crafts should be reconciled and that the practice of individual skills should permeate everyday life with the aim of producing objects of beauty and utility. Morris's dictum was to 'have nothing in your houses that you do not know to be useful, or believe to be beautiful'.

While Japan's artistic traditions had a profound effect upon France and Britain, Indonesia would influence Dutch design. The Javanese batik textiles were particularly valued by connoisseurs and artists alike for their unique, hand-skilled production. This perception of their value as craft objects was the decisive motivation for the introduction of batik to the Netherlands in the 1890s. A further factor was the exotic decorative patterns which became the direct inspiration for the 'Nieuwe Kunst' ('New Art') style.

The first European artist credited with the use of the batik technique was a student from Amsterdam, Leon Cachet. In 1891, he visited the collection of batik at the city's Ethnographical Museum and was so impressed that he produced some work on silk. His exhibits of batik the following year attracted considerable attention. With another prominent artist, Gerrit Dijsselhof, he developed a practical understanding of the elementary dye technology. They progressed by producing innovative

designs for interior panels and screens. Another distinctive artist, Thorn Prikker, took a different approach. As designer to the Arts & Crafts Gallery in The Hague, he opened a studio in 1897 to mass-produce abstract designs by using stencils.

The increasing interest of artists in batik was encouraged by the Colonial Museum in Haarlem. H A J Baaders, architect and keen batik artist, was employed in 1900 to carry out research at the Haarlem Laboratory which was attached to the Museum. He conducted many experiments into wax and dye compounds, adapting the traditional processes to European requirements. A specialized range of aniline dyes was developed. These were durable, light-fast and, most importantly, could be used at low temperature. The 'Haarlem Group' of artists co-operated and benefited; lectures and publications were made freely available to meet growing public demand.

Gerret Rouffaer visited Java and studied its culture between 1885 and 1890 and, subsequently, in 1910–12. He was considered the ultimate European authority on the aesthetic value of batik. Through his writings

Leon Cachet, 1894 (detail).

82 x 67 cm

(32 $^1/_4$ x 26 $^1/_1$ in).

Rijksmuseum Amsterdam.

and lectures he played a crucial role in the renaissance of Indonesian art in the Netherlands. He argued for the government to protect the batik economy in Java, while convincing the Museums in the Netherlands to show respect for their collection of authentic batiks. Displays were improved and artists were able to admire at close hand the finer qualities of the indigenous craft. Rouffaer was equally enthusiastic that Dutch artists should use the technique in innovative and artistic ways.

The principal and most influential artist to collaborate with the Haarlem Laboratory was Chris Lebeau. He was the first to combine the refined traditional Javanese technique with the Art Nouveau decorative style. Reviews praised his reinvigorating role in Dutch art, showing admiration at his 'feeling of the self', unfettered by the tradition-bound attitudes of Javanese culture. He lectured at the Applied Art School in Haarlem from 1904 to 1912, propagating batik's professional status and style. Many batik artists took up permanent teaching posts in Switzerland and Germany. A significant number of students who studied at the Haarlem Laboratory came from France and Belgium. Among the most successful enterprises was one created by Marguerite Pangon in Paris. In 1916 she established a studio employing 50 people creating and making designs for clothes, shawls, lampshades and fabrics. Her style was very influential during the 1920s and can be traced in the work of Erté, Leon Bakst and Sergei Diaghilev.

By 1900 batik had become a standard feature of arts and crafts exhibitions. It was promoted at the World Exposition in Paris in 1900, where it stimulated discussion and played a prize-winning role as an

Chris Lebeau. Detail of his typical style of batik.

innovative technique. This was followed in 1902 by further successes at the International Exhibition of Modern Decorative Arts in Turin.

Prior to 1910, batik was in the domain of the professional artist. Then, through the educational curriculum, batik began to become accessible to an increasing number of enthusiastic practitioners. It could be applied as decoration to lampshades, book covers and dress accessories. The Haarlem style was pre-eminent up to World War I, but a greater stylistic diversity can be seen from around 1920, with thousands of practitioners as far afield as the United States and Australia.

The end of an era for international acclaim came in the Exposition Internationale des Arts Décoratifs et Industriels Modernes, held in Paris in 1925, which signalled the advent of Art Deco. The change of aesthetic that followed favoured bolder, abstract patterning with contrasting colours, contrary to the flowing curves that characterized the Art Nouveau style of the Haarlem batiks. The faster mode of the Jazz age and, later, the deteriorating economic climate, also contributed to the decline of batik practice.

Batik's reappearance in the 1960s was prompted by the creative revolution of that decade in the West. Artists were exploring new materials and techniques. Everything was in continual motion, being tested and reinvented. Artists were eager to change all art forms, but it was precisely in the area called 'applied' that the changes were most liberating. The prospect of the wax-resist dyed fabric serving or reacting to an artistic concept was the challenge.

Sarong Semarang, cotton detail, 1860–1880. 203 x 106 cm (80 x 41 ³/₄ in). Collection Rudolf Smend, Cologne.

The two rows of elongated triangles are called tumpal. It is said that the design represents crocodile teeth and protects the wearer against evil.

TRADITIONAL JAVANESE BATIK

Indonesia occupies a very special place in the textile world. The islands were a crossroad of ancient migration – Buddhism, Hinduism and Islam have all profoundly affected Indonesia's sacred and secular life. Batik textiles reflected these influences in their patterns and techniques. The Chinese immigrants in particular brought to bear their trading expertise and culture. In 1602 the Dutch East India Trading Company was formed and became the foundation for Dutch Colonial Rule. *Batik belanda* was the name given to batiks made in Indo-European workshops between 1840 and 1940. These batiks shared a disciplined and European style of design, which was a departure from the classic line. Japan invaded the Dutch East Indies in 1942 and for the duration of the occupation demanded a new style more to their taste called *Hokokai*. Due to the shortage of cotton, labour-intensive and intricate designs resulted.

After President Sukarno established independence in 1945, democratization of design was instituted, so that batik patterns would no longer identify the social class of the wearer. However, in recent years, European dress has become the norm, except for formal occasions when traditional batik is worn by both men and women. The future of batik in Java may depend on designers and artists producing individual works for a selective clientele.

MATERIALS AND TOOLS

Cotton is the most common material used in the making of batik garments in Java. Cotton clothing was worn by the people of Java and northern

Sumatra as far back as the sixth and seventh centuries. There is evidence that during the Song dynasty in China (960–1279) cotton goods from Java were customarily offered as princely gifts. In the 15th century they were exported to islands west of Borneo. At one time fine cotton cloth was imported from India, but since 1815 this has been supplanted by European imports. Today Java is also producing cambric in four grades – primissima (the finest), prima, biru, and merah (the coarsest).

The cotton is cut to the required length and has then to be freed of its gelatinous sizing agent. It is thoroughly boiled and washed, soaked in a bath and kneaded well by hand or under foot, and then dried out of doors. The process that follows is known as mordanting, where the cloth is soaked in a mixture of oil and lye. Lye is obtained from the ashes of rice straw or the trunks of various types of banana plant. It is customarily mixed with castor oil or groundnut oil or, more rarely, with sesame oil. If the cloth is to be dyed red with morinda the process of mordanting may last as long as 40 days. If, however, the material is to be dyed indigo or brown, the cloth is boiled only in a diluted solution of rice paste, to which a little lime and bamboo leaves are added.

The cloth is then sized again to prevent the liquid wax from penetrating into the fibres too freely. The size used is usually a diluted paste of rice starch or cassava, sometimes with the addition of alum. The final process involves pounding the fabric with a wooden mallet. The resulting surface, rendered smooth and malleable, proves receptive to the drawing process which is the next stage in the production of batik.

Silk fabrics are mordanted in a bath of oil and lye for approximately two weeks but are not generally pre-washed. They are then spread on mats to dry, unlike cotton cloths, which are hung up on bamboo racks. They are subsequently sized. Silk is mostly reserved for the manufacture of *slendangs* (a shawl worn over the shoulder).

The waxing process, traditionally done by women, follows. The cloth is hung over wooden or bamboo frames, and the main divisions are outlined in charcoal or pencil. The experienced batik worker may now proceed to draw the traditional patterns from memory or copy them from a finished cloth hung beside her as a model. In some cases she may employ a parchment stencil or pattern called a *polas*, which she places beneath the fabric.

The instrument for the application of the wax is the *canting*. This consists of a small copper cup with one or more capillary spouts and a handle of reed or bamboo. The number of these spouts and their openings vary. For drawing outlines a canting with a very slender spout is used with which it is possible to draw a stroke about a millimetre ($\frac{1}{25}$ in) wide. For drawing designs consisting of a number of dots or lines at even distances, cantings with two to seven spouts are used. To cover small spaces, a cup with a broad spout is used, while large spaces are filled with a crude brush formed by fastening a wad of cloth to the mouth of the canting.

The wax traditionally used is beeswax, customarily obtained from Timor, Sumbawa or Sumatra. In 1860 it began to be replaced by a cheaper ozocerite (a naturally occuring waxy hydrocarbon) from Eastern

Europe, but since 1905 paraffin produced locally has replaced the ozocerite. Mixtures of beeswax, paraffin, micro crystalline wax, pine resin and animal fat are common today, and the recipes are often closely guarded secrets.

Heated in a pan of copper, iron or earthenware, the wax is maintained in a liquid state at as even a temperature as possible, over an open fire. This is done on a small brick stove of cylindrical form called an *anglo* with a square opening on one side and sometimes a removable lid on top. When the melted wax has been carefully brought to the correct temperature, the worker fills the canting. Care is taken not to touch the cloth with the canting while drawing, and great skill is required in handling the instrument. From the earliest recorded times the specialists in this work have been women.

When one side of the material is waxed, it is turned and hung over the rack against the sun to be reserved on the reverse side. This reserving process is done with various mixtures of wax – light and dark – so that the different sections of the design are clearly defined. Mixed waxes are strained through a cloth to prevent residue obstructing the smooth flow of the wax. Light wax is reserved for outlines and intricate designs, while large spaces are done with the darker mixtures. It may take a worker between 30 and 50 days to make a sarong 2 m (79 in) in length, depending on the complexity of the design. The most difficult work is divided among experienced batik workers, who concentrate on the production of intricate detail, while novices are employed on reserving the background.

Sarong Pekalongan, 1920 (detail).

Collection Rudolf Smend

Veining is not a common element in traditional batiks as it is considered an imperfection. In indigo dyeing, the cloth is exposed to the sun long enough to keep the wax supple.

Rice flower paste replaces beeswax as a resist on cotton and is traditionally dyed one colour – turkey red (*mengkudu*) – in more isolated districts in south-west Java. The quality of such batiks tends to be cruder than wax-resist cloth. Cotton cloth is mordanted for 40 days by being repeatedly boiled in oil and lye and then washed and dyed. It is then spread out horizontally between four pegs or laid flat on the ground. The surface is divided by small wooden sticks and the design drawn on with the rice paste. Occasionally, the designs are drawn with the fingers directly, with bamboo spoons or with a rag wrapped around a bamboo pin. For more intricate details bamboo quills are used. The dye, a cold turkey-red solution, is applied to the fabric with a broad brush. When the dyeing is completed, the paste is removed by soaking the whole cloth in cold water.

DYES AND DYEING METHODS

Natural indigo is the oldest dye traditionally used in Indonesia. It is also the only purely vat dye (one which is fixed by oxidation). Its use in the dyeing of fabrics also extends to Asia and Africa, and where batik has not developed beyond a primitive stage, indigo is invariably the only dyestuff that is employed.

The manufacture of indigo dyestuffs and the actual process of dyeing with indigo is also done by men. They add a coconut shell of natural indigo (obtained from plants such as *indigofera*) to a mixture of lime, sugar and water in a large container at midday. The mixture is stirred and left until the following morning when it is ready for use. If indigo white is required, sugar is added to transform the insoluble indigo blue into indigo white, which is soluble. Transformation comes about through a process of fermentation. To provide the necessary alkaline content, lime is added.

Dyeing starts in the early morning and is carried out in white, glazed receptacles. The cloths are steeped for two to three hours, dried in the air and then steeped again. During this process, it is imperative that the cloths are completely covered by the liquid dye or small spots may appear. The dyeing process lasts for six to ten days, depending on the strength of colour required. Occasionally, the process may take even longer, though methods of shortening it have been devised. If, for example, the fabric is treated with a solution of finely pounded bark of *Rhizophoracea ceriops candolleana* (a species of mangrove) after each dipping, the process may be further accelerated. If synthetic indigo is used with an addition of ferrous sulphate and lime, the process may be shortened to two days. If a black colour is desired, repeated dyeing with indigo will achieve the required result. An alternative method is to cover a dark indigo with brown.

Women traditionally carry out the red and brown dyeing. The dyestuff used for red is a mixture of dyer's morinda (the root bark of *Morinda citrifolia L.*) and the bark of *Symplocos fasciculata zoll*, in the proportion of 1:1 or 2:1. The fabric, which has previously been mordanted in oil and ash lye, is placed in a flat receptacle, and the dye is poured over it. The dye is rubbed in by hand, and this process is repeated for 24 days.

The dyestuff for browns is more variable. Usually it consists of the bark of the soga tree, the tingi tree, or the 'yellow wood', also known as tegerang. In the Yogyakarta area, varnishing resin, colophonium and sugar are added to these, but gambier and sugar are added in Semarang. Repeated steaming and additions of water dissolve the ingredients. Dyeing in the case of browns takes place in lukewarm water, unlike blue and red dyeing, which is always cold. The temperature must not exceed 45° C (112° F) as this would melt the layer of wax. This process lasts between one and eight days. Brown colours have to be fixed. This is generally done in plain lime water, but for finer work special substances are used. These determine the different shades of brown and are generally well-guarded secrets. In the main, they contain various proportions of saltpetre, alum, quicklime, borax, lemon juice and crystalline sugar.

In the past it was possible to identify the batiks of different regions by their distinctive colours. For example, the batiks of Yogyakarta were distinguished by their clear, bright whites; those of Surakarta by their softer creams. Both regions are traditionally limited to dark blue and brown colours. The batiks of Indramayu were noted for combinations of blue and black and those of Pekalongan for their vivid and varied colours, while Cirebon batiks were famous for their landscape designs on a rich ivory background. Now, however, the use of synthetic indigo, alizarin (for red), auramines and aniline has wiped out the distinctions brought about

by local variations in dyestuffs and procedures.

Before synthetic dyes became available, the natural colourants were indigo, turkey red from morinda, and yellow from curcuma and cudriana. Greens were obtained by over-dyeing light blue with yellow, and black, as already explained, by repeatedly dyeing with indigo or over-dyeing dark indigo with brown. The predominance of delicate and subdued shades in traditional batiks was, to a large extent, the consequence of a restricted number of dyestuffs from natural sources and their tendency to fade rapidly when exposed to tropical sunlight.

Today, as a result of the introduction of artificial colourants, this subtlety of colouring is no longer the main characteristic of the batik art of Indonesia, though the old cloths are still treasured and sought after.

Soga Kerokan Method

The principles of batik are the same, but the step-by-step procedures vary according to the region. In central Java the best-known method is called *soga kerokan*. The following steps show the principle most clearly:

1. The cloth is first cut into traditional length for a batik, known as a *kain*, 250 x 105 cm (98 x 41 in), which is then hemmed to prevent fraying.
2. Manufactured cloth has usually been treated and therefore it has to be washed and rinsed and washed again until clear.
3. Starch made of rice or cassava is applied so that the wax will adhere more readily to a smooth and firm surface. In addition, the cloth is oiled for extra-fine work, to give greater wax control.

Drawing in wax with a tool known as canting. It is an ingenious Javanese invention, discovered in the 17th century at the Court of Mataram.

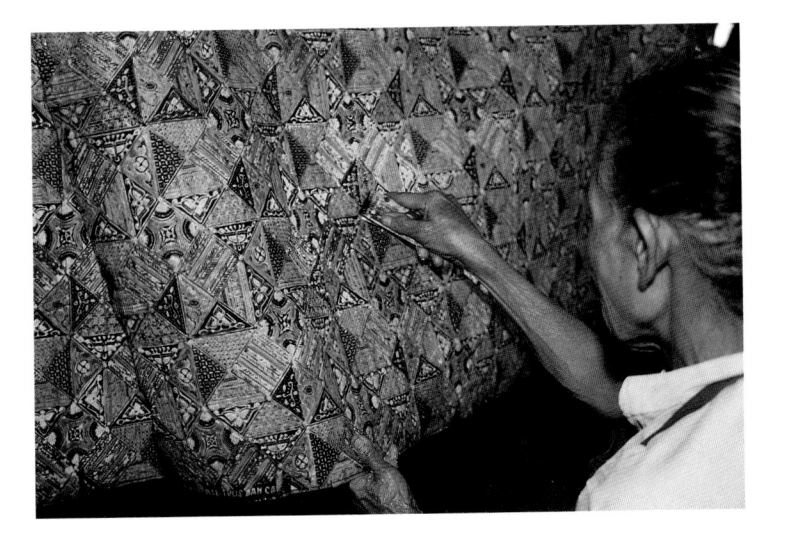

4. The cloth is beaten with a mallet to make it more supple.

5. Once the motifs are learnt, the batik worker draws the wax on to the cloth from memory.

6. Two types of wax are applied to the cloth in the first waxing: *klowong* wax is light and brittle and will be easily removed after the first dyeing; *tembok* wax is stronger and will remain on the finished cloth to reserve the white areas of the design. Because the cloth will be dyed repeatedly, the wax must be extremely resistant and flexible and would be considered inferior work if it broke down or marbled.

7. The reverse of the cloth is also waxed exactly to the design to ensure that the colour is completely protected and clear in the finished cloth.

8. Dyeing with indigo is a tradition that is passed from father to son. The making of the dye has all kinds of superstitions attached to it, and the process is a sacred ritual. The cloth is dipped between 20 and 60 times, suspended from a rack that usually holds about 20 waxed batiks at one time. The item is exposed for 15 minutes to oxidize before redipping. It is a very long and complex procedure and takes many days before the right depth of colour appears. After repeated use, the dye becomes weak and needs revitalizing by the addition of indigo paste, iron vitriol and lime.

9. After dyeing, the brittle klowong wax is removed by the batik worker who first soaks the cloth in cold water to harden the wax. A scraper made of tin or a knife takes the wax off both surfaces. The white parts of the design are now exposed for the next dyeing, whilst the stickier wax

Scraping wax off part of the pattern to expose it to further dye colour.

remains to protect the white pattern throughout the successive dips.

10. The cloth is rinsed in cold water to remove any klowong wax on its surface. A little soda is added to free any residue.

11. Before the final dyeing in soga, a second waxing is applied to the indigo blue areas to protect the colour. Where the brown overdyes the exposed blue, it will create black. For this stage a third kind of wax is used called *biron* which need not have the flexibility or brittle quality of the previous waxing. It is usually made of scraps of boiled-off wax for economy as it has to survive only for the final dyeing.

Besides the indigo blue being covered with wax to compound the design, repairs are made to the tembok wax. If any breaks have occurred during handling, a heated nail is applied to fuse the wax together.

12. The cloth is washed carefully and finally dyed in the brown known as soga.

13. The soga vat is smaller than the indigo vat and each piece is dipped by hand. The pieces are dipped between 15 and 30 times and finally fixed.

14. The finished waxed and dyed cloth is then placed in a cauldron of boiling water containing soda ash or caustic soda to remove the wax. After the cloth has been agitated with a stick, the wax floats to the surface and is scooped off and recycled.

15. Once the wax is removed, the cloth is then finished by being washed thoroughly in a soapy solution.

Removing the dyed wax cloth from the bath.

Pekalongan Method

Since the introduction of synthetic dyes, an old technique has been revived for producing multicoloured contemporary batik. Originally, the painted-on technique was introduced from India, but was replaced by the rewaxing and overdyeing processes to produce many-coloured combinations. The method, called *coletan*, does not require the cloth to be dipped for each colour. As the wax does not have to be removed after each dyeing, the process is much quicker and more predictable. Outlines of wax are drawn around motifs, and indigosol dyes are brushed directly into them; the wax prevents bleeding of the colour. These motifs are then sealed, and the background colour is dipped or, alternatively, left the ground colour of the cloth. The procedure is as follows:

1. Prepare cloth, and pencil in the design.
2. Wax outlines of motif and cover areas that will eventually be dyed brown.
3. Select and brush in colours within wax borders.
4. Wax coloured areas.
5. Immerse cloth in indigo or intended background colour.
6. Remove wax by immersion in boiling water.
7. Wax all areas except those to be dyed brown.
8. Immerse cloth in soga brown.
9. Finally remove wax in boiling water.

Boiling out wax.

CAP PRINTING

Most Javanese batiks are stamp-printed today for economy. In the mid-19th century the cap revolutionized the production of batiks and turned it into a thriving industry.

The making of the cap is an individual craft: it involves cutting out the patterns from rolls of sheet copper and attaching them to a frame so that they form a level impression when applied to the cloth.

The repetitive quality of the stamp designs can be distinguished from the hand-drawn ones. However, to the layman the difference is not easy to define, particularly if the patterns are made up of many small interrelated stamps. Sometimes as many as 16 are used and usually pairs of stamps are made for printing on both sides of the cloth. Mirror image fitting is essential for registration and clarity. Different compositions of wax-resist also require separate blocks.

Pekalongan batik. It shows the combination of the wax outline technique and selective colour application.

Cap printing is carried out on an angled table which is padded and kept moist by applying a diluted lye solution. This ensures that the wax does not stick to the table when the stamp is applied. The wax is heated in a pan containing a porous cushion, which soaks up any impurities in the wax that may spoil the printing. The cap printer dips the stamp into the wax pan, then lifts and taps off any excess wax that may clog the pattern. The temperature has to be judged correctly before the stamp is applied to the cloth, edge-on first for registration. Full pressure is then applied and the stamp released when the impression has been made. After completing one side, the cloth is reversed and the matching wax stamps are applied to confirm a complete resist. According to custom, this work is done by men.

TRADITIONAL PATTERNS

The greatest variety of batik patterns stems from Java. Many were decreed by the Sultans of Yogyakarta and Surakarta in the 18th century to be sacred to the Royal Family and could be worn only by them. There are at least a thousand patterns that can be exactly defined and bear names such as moonshine charm, boar at night and waddling goose. These patterns are an amalgamation of ornamentations drawn from a wide variety of periods and places, including India, China, Japan and, in the case of more modern batiks, Europe. The patterns can be classified within four basic types:

Cap printing.

This pattern usually reveals a non-Javanese influence in natural shapes such as leaves and flowers combined, either in pairs or singly, with the *lar* or wing motif, which is round, and the mountain and cloud motif, believed to be Chinese in origin.

Ceplok

This is a continuous symmetrical pattern of natural units seen from above and formed into circles and squares based on a microscopic observation of natural forms. These stars, rosettes and crosses are generally arranged in symmetrical groups such as the *ganggong*. The names of such patterns, despite their formalized appearance, point to their origin in natural forms.

Another form of ceplokken design is based on the patterns formed by plaited or woven fabrics or fibres. The effect here is achieved by a series of dots and dashes placed at regular intervals.

Parang

This slanting diagonal stripe pattern contains smaller geometrical floral repeat patterns. These motifs were generally reserved for the garments of princes, nobles and court officials. This had to be faultlessly drawn as a flaw would destroy the power imbued in the cloth.

Kawung

This motif is composed of a series of ellipses or ovals arranged in groups

Javanese dancer wearing a *Parang* pattern sarong.

of four, looking like a simplified lotus. The cross in the centre represents a universal source of energy. It is a very ancient pattern derived from Persia and connected with forbidden ornaments.

Perhaps the oldest known Indonesian design is the *gringsing* or fish-scale pattern, usually employed as a background. True to the dictates of Islam the human figure does not appear, with the exception of those occasions when figures from the *wayang* plays are used, and here the fish-scale pattern customarily appears as the background.

A strange horned animal with scales occurs in the batik work of northern Java and is thought to be Chinese in origin, while the phoenix and the fish – a Chinese symbol of fertility – appear in Cirebon batiks. In more recent times in northern Java batiks depicting scenes of native life have appeared. Again, these could be ascribed to Chinese influences.

In most other parts of the world the patterns are less varied than in Indonesia. Many of them are confined to the use of indigo and white and most are geometric and far simpler in design than Indonesian motifs.

TRADITIONAL GARMENTS

To some extent ornamentation in batik is dictated by the type of garment for which it is designed.

Kepala

A large head cloth about 1 m (39 in) square, this is worn only by men. It is customarily decorated with motifs distributed over its entire surface, but at the centre there is a plain diamond shape which is left undyed in contrast to the patterned frame, although occasionally it is dyed plain indigo, red or yellow. This diamond is sometimes framed by a frieze of *cemukirans,* or small pointed leaves which alter from district to district. Occasionally, too, the border of the garment imitates a fringe.

Kemben and Slendang

These are long shawl-like cloths of about 50–250 cm (20–98 in) in size. Javanese dancers wear sashes which are slightly narrower. The *kemben* is a breast cover which is rarely worn today, but the more traditional *slendang* is slung over one shoulder and is often used to carry babies or provisions. Traditionally, these cloths are covered entirely with patterns though they may also have an unpatterned rectangle in the centre. If the pattern takes the form of an elongated lozenge, the cloth is known as *blumbangan* and has straight or scalloped sides. Alternatively, if it is a rectangle the same shape as the cloth, it is called *sundangen.* These cloths are decorated with borders and the central lozenge or rectangle is defined by cemukiran motifs.

Sarong

This is a waist cloth, used by both men and women. It is on this garment that the traditional arrangement of the ornaments is most significant. The sarong covers the body and legs from the waist down to the ankles and may be made of cotton or silk fabric. It is about 107 x 189 cm (41 x 74 in) in size. It is either wrapped around the hips and thus secured, or sewn into the shape of an open sack into which the wearer steps. This garment is drawn tight on one side and fastened upon itself in a knot or secured with a belt.

The ornamentation of the sarong is divided into three parts: the centre piece called the *kepala*, flanked by two large wings. The kepala carries a strictly geometric design which remains the same on all sarongs and the two wings are more elaborately decorated. The kepala contains two rows of narrow triangles with points facing one another and is framed on each side by narrow borders called *papam* or *cumpak*. The top and bottom seams of the sarong are bordered by a very narrow ornamented stripe. The designs on the side parts vary from district to district. They may have a different pattern at each end called *pagi–sore*, meaning morning–evening. By folding the cloth in different ways, its use can be altered.

Kain

This is a longer, more formal cloth than the sarong, and is also used by both men and women. The entire cloth is decorated with borders at the short ends; it is wrapped around the waist, with the last 50 cm (20 in) arranged as pleats at the back of the body.

Dodot

This is larger than the sarong and up to twice as long. With a plain lozenge-shaped centre surrounded by even patterning, *dodots* are worn with a train or a large hanging fold on the side. This is a formal garment, worn by princes, court dancers, high officials and wedding couples.

Adrift Noel Dyrenforth

136 x 165 cm (53 $\frac{1}{2}$ x 65 in).

Wax-resist, reactive/discharged dyed cotton, 2001

MODERN BATIK

The contemporary batik artist, setting up a workshop, will have access to appropriate materials and tools and, since the requirements are few, should acquire and employ only the very best in respect of quality. With perseverance, the development of manual skills and an imaginative approach to the craft, the artist can enjoy the unique value that this medium offers for self-expression.

THE WORKSHOP

The first requirement in setting up a workshop is, of course, space. Where a workshop is by necessity small, great care should be taken in planning the area so that it yields the maximum efficiency in production and safety. An ideal set-up is a fully equipped, self-contained workshop, though this often means resorting to making the best of a domestic living area.

- Natural light is a prime requirement as it makes fine judgements of colour possible; in its absence, good even electric lighting is essential.
- Ventilation must also be given careful consideration as wax fumes can cause irritation. An efficient electric extractor fan is the best solution.
- The working surfaces themselves must be smooth, stable and durable. Plastic sheeting on the floor provides a protective surface.
- The workshop should, if possible, have a liberal supply of electric points – either wall-mounted or overhead leads of the track variety for connection to wax heaters, fans, and so on.

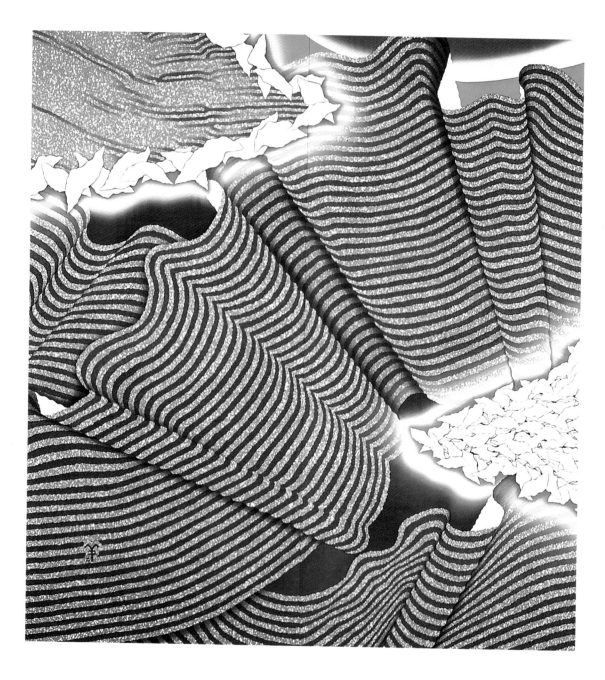

- A large sink with a supply of hot and cold water is a necessity.
- Airtight containers to store dyes away from heat and light are useful; for safety as well as information, they should be clearly labelled and dated.
- A supply of bowls, heatproof measuring jugs and measuring spoons is essential. For dip-dyeing, shallow plastic baths are recommended as they are inexpensive and easy to manipulate.
- To heat the wax, a thermostatically controlled container is the most practical and safe solution.
- A good-quality measuring scale, preferably with scale (0–500 g or 0–17$^2/_3$ oz) is necessary.
- A drying area away from direct sunlight is also needed.

Safety Precautions

Confident and practical safety precautions ensure that the artist can work in a relaxed and uninhibited manner. Maintain a good working practice when handling or storing dyestuffs and chemicals. Wear protective clothing including gloves and mask. By law, dye and chemical suppliers issue safety instructions. Generally avoid any inhalation of powder or fumes. If dyes or chemicals touch the skin or eyes, wash in cold water immediately. It would be sensible to keep a first-aid box in the workshop.

Extra care should also be taken with heating wax. Excessive fumes are a health hazard. Thermostatic pots ensure that the wax does not get overheated. In the absence of an extractor fan, be sure to have plenty of natural ventilation.

Yo Shoukoh Kobayashi
150 x 700 cm (59 x 274 in).
Wax-resist, acid dyed
on silk, 1999.

Yo Shoukoh Kobayashi
150 x 140 cm (59 x 55 in).
Wax-resist, acid dyed on silk.

FABRICS

For the best result, cloth made from natural fibres is recommended. The only man-made fibre that can be considered for use in the production of batiks is Viscose Rayon.

Cotton

Cotton, either wild or cultivated, has been in use as a textile fibre for several thousands of years. One fragment known to be 3000 years old, of Indian origin, has survived and it is generally supposed that India was the birthplace of cotton fabric. However, cotton was also used at a very early stage in Egypt – some authorities claim as early as 12,000 BC. In North America, cotton was first cultivated in the state of Virginia in 1607, becoming the mainstay of the economy of the southern United States in the following century. With Eli Whitney's invention in 1793 of the cotton gin, a machine that facilitated the extraction of the seeds from raw cotton, production became possible on an ever-grander scale.

Cotton is a hair attached to the seed of several species of the genus *Gossypium*, a shrub that grows between 120 and 180 cm (4 and 6 ft) high and is indigenous to nearly all tropical regions. It flourishes near the sea, lakes or large rivers where there is a warm, humid climate and sandy soil. Today, the main cotton-producing areas are Egypt, the southern United States, India, Brazil, Turkey, the west coast of Africa, the Caribbean, Russia and China. The best crops are obtained by cultivating the plants annually.

Edge Noel Dyrenforth

127 x 95 cm (50 x 37 ¹/₂ in).

Wax-resist, reactive/discharged dyed cotton, 1993.

Each cotton fibre has 20–30 layers of cellulose built up in an orderly series of spring-like spirals. When the cotton ball opens, the fibres dry into flat, twisted, ribbon-like shapes and become interlocked. This makes an ideal form for spinning into fine yarn. These characteristics of the fibre account for the durability, absorbency, wet-strength and softness of cotton. Because the fibre is hollow, it can absorb a great deal of moisture. The outer layer of cellulose contains a wax which gives surface smoothness and a natural lustre to the fabric. It is therefore an ideal material for subjecting to the action of dyes as the fibres can scarcely be damaged by their action.

An immense variety of cloths are manufactured from cotton: voile,

Adjustable wooden frame and fabric.

organdie, lawn, satin, poplin, pique, corduroy, velvet, repp, denim and gabardine among them.

Linen

In Egypt and the Near East, the use of linen was established by 3000 BC. It is woven from yarn made from the fibres of the flax plant, a member of the family *Linaceae*. The flax plant grows best in temperate climates, free from heavy rains, but where moist winds occur during the growing season. Flax is still grown in Ireland at Bunclody. Most of the fibre used in the linen industry in Ireland, however, is imported from France and the republics of the former Soviet Union. The Russian fibre is inferior in quality for textile use as it is short and strong.

Flax is not cut but is pulled from the ground when the green stems begin to turn yellow. Today this process is performed entirely by machines. After disposing of the woody part of the stem, the flax is dried and then beaten or scutched to break the pith and free the fibres with as little damage as possible.

The best fibre is pale yellow in colour, flexible and lustrous, though by comparison with cotton yarn, linen is more irregular and less pliant, which causes it to crease more easily.

Silk

The Chinese held a monopoly on silk production for about 3,000 years, although it is possible that India produced silk as early as 1000 BC. The

Ascend Noel Dyrenforth

50 x 50 cm (19 $^2/_3$ x 19 $^2/_3$ in).

Silk/paper. Wax-resist, reactive/discharged dyed, 2001.

secret of sericulture was smuggled out of China by two Persian monks who disguised themselves as Christian missionaries and transported a small quantity of silkworm eggs out of the country in hollow cane. The secrets they had gathered about silk production were given to the Emperor Justinian who proclaimed a monopoly on the trade in 552. Arabs brought this knowledge to Sicily and Italy, and for centuries Lucca in northern Italy was the centre of the European silk-weaving industry. By the 13th century Lyon and Tours in France were also established silk-weaving areas.

The main source of silk today is the Chinese moth *Bombyx mori*. This is an ash-coloured moth whose caterpillar feeds on mulberry leaves, converting the albumen content of the leaves into liquid silk which it stores in its body. Silk is extruded through two spinnerets on either side of the head and a cocoon is thus formed. If the moth is allowed to emerge from the cocoon in the normal way, the threads are damaged. Accordingly, the cocoons are hot-air dried to kill the insect within. The outer part of the cocoon is then discarded and the middle section boiled to soften the gum which seals it. The end of the thread is then located and the silk wound onto a frame. The average silkworm produces about 1,800 m (2,000 yd) of thread, but only about 450 m (500 yd) are used as continuous filament. The other silk-producing moths, found mostly in Asia, live on oak and other leaves and produce tussah, chantung and honan, which are all wild silks.

Natural silk is one of the strongest textile fibres, having a stretched-out molecular form. Once degummed, it has a tensile strength of 4–5 g per denier. By contrast, softened steel has a rate of 3 g. Silk fibres can be extended to up to 25 per cent of their length before breaking. Silk is available in a wide variety of textures and weights; the smooth type is best for batik.

Wool

Wool has been spun and woven by man from as early as the seventh century BC. Wool and hair are fibres of protein which emerge from the hair follicles coated with grease.

Fleeces sheared during the warm season contain 43–50 per cent wool by weight (the remaining weight comprises oils, fats, moisture and dirt). Wool fibre is enclosed in irregular overlapping scales with cell tissue inside them. The outer cuticle is resistant to wetting, but moisture in vapour form can be absorbed by the fibres.

There are hundreds of wool fabrics, but for batik the best are crêpe, jersey, lightweight plain weaves such as Liberty varuna and mixtures such as Viyella.

PREPARATION OF FABRICS

Today, most commercially available fabrics have already been scoured to remove foreign matter and bleached to be as white as possible. Before work can be carried out, however, it is advisable to test the fabric for dye-absorption and streaking. If there are indications that the fabric contains impurities it will then be necessary to pre-treat it before work starts on the batik process. In many cases, a good soak in warm water, followed by thorough rinsing, may be sufficient; alternatively, the fabric may be

machine-washed. The fabric must be rinsed thoroughly and ironed while still damp.

In immersion-dyeing, this scouring process is perhaps not quite so vital as the long period in the dye bath ensures that the dye penetrates the fibres. In brush or spray dyeing, however, when the period of absorption is necessarily far shorter, scrupulous scouring is essential.

If silk has to be treated it is necessary to exercise the greatest care. The silk should be soaked in water at a temperature of 70° C (158° F) for about 30 minutes. Three per cent soda ash may be added to the water and the addition of a little white vinegar to the final rinse should ensure that the fabric is freed of all impurities. A water softener is also a good addition and renders the fabric more receptive to the dyes.

WAX

The quality of the resist depends primarily on the composition and diverse nature of the waxes available. It can come from many sources, including plants, animals and minerals as well as synthetic materials.

Waxes: micro crystalline, paraffin, beeswax, resins for special recipes and standard mixes of micro crystalline and paraffin are readily available, as are thermostatically controlled wax heaters.

Beeswax, traditionally used, is strong and durable but is not resistant to alkaline and can cause unresolved breaks when dyed.

Micro crystalline wax, a synthetic with similar properties, is flexible and penetrates the fabric easily. It is resistant to dye penetration and does not easily crack. An inexpensive substitute for beeswax.

Paraffin wax has a lower melting point than micro crystalline wax, is thin and tends to crack and flake off the material.

Resin used in resist dyeing comes from the pine tree and is hard and sticky, but also cracks very easily. It has a high melting point and is often added to other waxes to increase viscosity.

Fat has a very low melting point, is greasy and contributes a greater flexibility to a recipe.

Stearin wax is sold in white flake form and usually has a low melting point. Its ability to resist dye is weak and it does not adhere to the cloth well, so it is rarely used on its own. Excellent for mixing with stickier wax for fluidity.

Damor gum is not a wax but a gum suspended in a volatile oil. Used in conjunction with the basic formula to obtain half-resist effects.

One can vary formulas and experiment by adding a little of this and that. With experience, it will become possible to control these proportions to obtain the desired outcome. A word of caution, however: paraffin wax is brittle and doesn't adhere to the cloth well; used on its own it could cause the dye to undermine the imagery. Preparation of the recipes is crucial to the result.

A commercial, ready-made batik wax consists of paraffin and micro crystalline waxes in the ratio of 2:1. This usually comes in a granulated form and is recommended for general use.

Wax tools: a selection from Japan, Sri Lanka, Malaysia, the Ukraine and Europe.

WAX RECIPES

Here are some resist-wax recipes to try:

- *General purpose wax*: 1 part beeswax; 1 part micro crystalline wax; 1 part paraffin.
- *Strong wax suitable for canting*: 6 parts pine resin; 4 parts paraffin; 1 part beeswax; 0.25 part damor gum; 0.25 part fat.
- *Blocking wax for covering areas*: 2 parts beeswax; 1 part pine resin; 0.5 part damor gum; 0.5 part micro crystalline wax; 0.1 part fat.
- *Crackle wax – brittle for marble effects*: 5 parts paraffin wax; 5 parts pine resin; 1 part damor gum; 0.2 part fat.

The subtlety and strength of the wax resistance to the over-dyeing sequences can be controlled by the following:

- Composition and amount of different waxes.
- Temperature, which affects the level of wax penetration into the cloth.
- Style of application, whether with brush, canting, block, spray, and so on.

Method

Add the ingredients one by one, from the highest melting point to the lowest:

Damor gum 80° C (176° F)

Pine resin 80° C (176° F)

Micro crystalline wax 75° C (167° F)

Beeswax 58° C (136° F)

Paraffin 50° C (122° F)

Fat 50° C (122° F)

Wax tools from China and Indonesia (left).

Cleaning wax off exterior (right).

Safety Precautions

- Do not overheat wax as it may ignite. Maintain a temperature of about 120° C (248° F).
- Should fire occur, smother pot of wax with lid or douse with bicarbonate of soda.
- Keep away from an open flame. Clean hot-plate regularly of overspilt wax.
- Use extractor fan or ensure good ventilation.

THE WAX POT

To melt the wax, a substantial metal pan or pot, thermostatically controlled, with a stable base is needed. Care has to be taken that the wax does not overheat or it will smoke. An electric frying pan is also very practical as it is low and shallow and can accommodate a number of individual cans of different waxes.

It is important to maintain a constant temperature of about 120° C (248° F). The wax must be hot enough to penetrate the cloth to form a reliable resist against the dye. Overheating of the 'fatty' content in the wax will reduce its properties. Impurities in the wax can be filtered off by pouring through a muslin cloth.

TOOLS

There are a number of tools used for applying molten wax to cloth. The canting and brush are the traditional tools associated with batik, while block stamps and rollers with surfaces adapted for the retention of wax

Cleaning the spout with fuse wire.

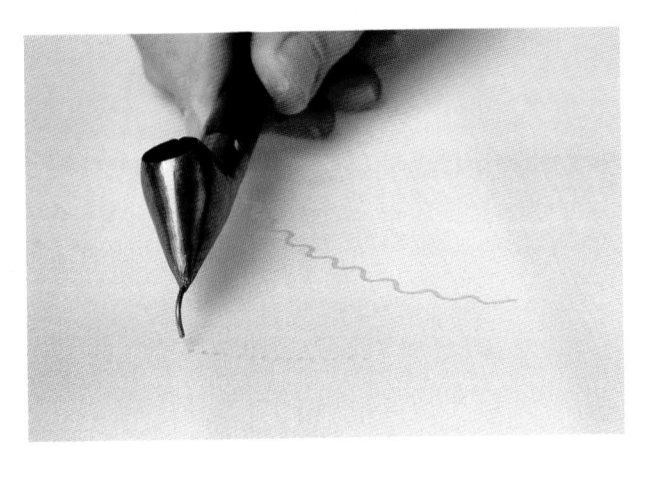

are associated with printing fabric. More random methods of applying wax such as splattering have now found their place in batik-making. It is important to keep tools in good working order.

Cantings

The canting is a small, spouted metal cup for applying wax. It comes in many sizes and may have up to seven spouts. The cantings are essentially used for drawing lines or dots. A canting is like a pen and may be employed to create the most intricate and refined designs; as such it is an indispensable tool. The cantings of Javanese origin have yet to be bettered technologically.

Handling the canting is a matter of some skill, but almost anyone can become adept at regulating the even flow of wax by following a few rules that make for good work practice.

- Ensure unrestrained working posture with easy access to wax pot.
- Hold the canting in a relaxed position, saddled between the forefinger and the thumb.
- When filling the canting, keep it in the molten wax until it is hot enough to allow the wax to flow consistently from the spout.
- Fill to only the halfway mark to avoid spilling wax over the work.
- Have a ready supply of absorbent material to wipe the spout and base of the cup before applying to the cloth.
- When drawing, handle the canting so that it is horizontal to the fabric.

Wax dots with canting.

The River Peter Wenger

130 x 160 cm (51 x 63 in).

Wax-resist indigo dyed cotton, 1997.

- Draw the tip of the spout slightly above the surface to release a smooth and consistent flow of wax. By pressing the canting on the cloth, the flow is blocked and penetration becomes unreliable.
- Steady your hand by using the little finger as a stabilizer.
- Work from left to right when drawing a straight line handed.
- Complete a circle in two half movements to ensure continuity of line.
- When 'dotting', work rhythmically.
- Refill before the wax is too cool to penetrate the cloth. This can be judged by the opaque quality of the wax.
- If the flow of wax is impeded by impurities, use a small piece of fuse wire to unblock the spout.
- If you wish to slow the flow of wax for more control, cool it by blowing into the spout.

Brushes for Waxing

Adaptable, heat-resistant natural-hair brushes enable the artist to handle the medium of hot wax with dexterity. For filling in large-patterned areas, a broad brush of good-quality natural hair or bristle is recommended. This will ensure that as much wax as possible is drawn up by the large brush to give greater coverage. Generally, a stiff brush, for instance one made of hog hair, is better than a soft one as it will force the wax more vigorously into the fabric. For finer work that can rival the quality of the canting line, a round hair brush with a flexible point can be handled either with precision or an expressive fluency. A Chinese or Japanese *sumi*-style brush is ideal

A selection of brushes suitable for waxing.

as it has a full head to act as a reservoir serving its fine point. Care should be taken not to damage or distort the brushes, especially the finer, more fragile hair-type. New brushes should be initiated by gradually acquainting them with the heated wax and by immersing them without touching the hot metal of the pot. The brush should be stroked into shape as the wax cools.

Once brushes are in constant use, they should not be left in the wax as they will rapidly burn and become misshapen and consequently difficult to use. Wax-impregnated brushes should never be left to harden against a work surface and should be kept regularly pruned of burnt bristles and reshaped before the wax hardens.

Brush-waxing techniques and speed of application come with practice. Crucial to the result is the temperature of the wax. To ensure a thorough resist, so that the dye liquid is repelled completely, penetration of the hot wax should be instant; cool wax is liable to become undermined or lift off during dyeing. Conversely, wax that is too hot will lose the adhesion and be difficult to control, diffusing and weakening the image. However, skilful manipulation of the temperature can blend and layer wax to create a range of effects from gossamer to graphic. The quality of a batik is much dependent on the intimate knowledge and skills in handling hot wax. In addition to the tools mentioned above, foam rubber can be cut and adapted to painting on wax very effectively.

Brushes for Dyeing

Brushes are used extensively in dyeing. There are three basic techniques: background or all-over dyeing; fill-in colour for individual segments; blending and shading. Brush dyeing allows much more choice than immersion dyeing. The best brushes are made of natural hair, tightly packed and absorbent. The Japanese textile artist has, by tradition, brushes that have been developed for dedicated use, the quality of which is unparalleled in the West.

For overall dyeing, a wide, full, short-haired brush which holds a reserve of dye without spilling or streaking on the cloth is the most efficient. The brush is moved swiftly back and forth, overlapping slightly, as it progresses over the cloth. As it is recharged with dye it is important to shake out any excess and to continue with a sweeping motion. The cloth is dried in a level position to avoid an uneven result.

A good-quality decorating brush up to 13 cm (5 in) wide or a foam-backed painting pad will substitute. For small areas of colour, watercolour brushes can be employed effectively by using a small circular motion. Each time the brush is recharged, it should be placed over the already coloured area to ensure even dyeing.

For shading, two brushes are generally used. First a fill-in brush, made of soft hair or foam, is applied, followed by a short, flat brush, used dry to feather the edge of the dye into the ground colour. This can be made by cutting down a watercolour brush to a flat stubble.

After use, brushes can be rinsed thoroughly in a mild detergent, shaken vigorously and dried. Clean brushes command clean colours.

Brushes for dyeing made of soft, absorbent hair or sponge.

Other Applications

Spray dyeing offers a subtle speckle effect, often used in conjunction with stencils and wax. The equipment ranges from a simple toothbrush and bottle spray to a compressor air gun. Stamps or blocks for wax prints can be made from any absorbent or heat-conductive material, such as metal, wood, felt, foam or cork. By using rollers wrapped with fine cotton, the hot wax will produce variable textural qualities.

COLOUR AND DESIGN

To produce effective colours and integrate them into a design, it is important to understand three variables – fabric, wax and dye – by working in an explorative manner. Observation of the spontaneous interaction between these elements will provide an insight into the nature and characteristics of batik.

Certain rules and techniques have to be considered and developed. The dye colour, absorbed by fabric and repelled by resist, is the essential, distinctive factor that defines the art of batik.

In pursuing the art form, you should aim to:

- Explore the effects.
- Approach everything without preconception and enjoy the experience of applying brush strokes of molten wax.
- Try out the refining skills of the canting by applying flowing lines of wax across stretched white cotton.

Adding wax during the design process.

- Pour primary dye colours on and see the resist perform.
- Watch the colours move and flow together creating spectrums of fresh unpremeditated pattern.

The waxing effects depend on the tools employed. Speed and dexterity will develop with increased experience. The choice of fabric and its woven structure will also be a factor, especially in its ability to absorb colour or reflect light. The artist's sensibilities will soon come into play, challenging preconception and revealing the medium's nature and creative promise.

Colour

The batik artist delights in a colour language. The educated eye learns to register and perceive a wide spectrum of transparent dye colour. To use colour in the most effective way, it is essential that the artist learns to anticipate the outcomes of different overdyeing sequences.

The first dye bath determines the direction of the overall colour plan. Dyestuffs each have their own characteristics, depending on the chemical process involved and the skill with which they are administered, which can give added depth and tone to a batik. For instance, reactive dyes cannot always give the intensity that naphthol dyes produce. For this reason, dyes should be tested on strips of fabric, which should be filed with the recipes that produced them, for future reference.

- It is useful to know how colour is categorized.
- *Primary colours*: the primary colours are red, yellow and blue which, when judiciously mixed together, can produce the whole spectrum of colour.
- *Secondary colours*: orange, green and violet. These are made by mixing two primary colours (for instance, violet is produced by mixing blue and red).
- *Intermediate colours*: mixtures of primary and secondary colours.
- *Complementary colours*: opposite colours on the spectrum (such as orange and blue).
- *Colour properties*: these terms are used to describe colour character.
- *Hue*: a pure colour. The value of colour is altered by the addition of black or water.
- *Intensity*: measured by the amount of light in a colour, that is the ratio of dye to water.

Design

Design is rooted in the real world of observation and it involves a process of selection and emphasis. One can draw on available sources, but a personal attitude is more valuable and inspirational. It is important to work within one's own ability and to avoid being too ambitious at first.

Photographs are a good source of design motifs as they are essentially objects already reduced to flat patterns. Furthermore, framing certain parts of a picture by masking off the rest serves to isolate sections and

Brushing dye over waxed cloth.

creates strong images. Focus on colour, texture and form in isolation from the overall design and, when designing with a function in mind, such as a garment, it should be remembered that the pattern or design has to be conceived as part of a three-dimensional form.

In this context, certain attitudes can be established which can fuel the imagination:

- Try to keep a sense of your own style, so your work is not a slavish copy of something you have seen.
- Try to keep your perceptions sharp so you can grasp the harmony of relationships between different elements of your design.
- Capitalize on the unique properties of batik, and be exuberant with the technique.
- Learn to respect the tools and materials and be confident in handling them.
- Remember that mistakes always happen; do not be so careful in your design that you set goals or rules that subjugate self-expression.
- Change and challenge should motivate the artist's concepts.

Sammal-1 Shigeki Fukumoto

145 x 145 cm (57 x 57 in).

Wax-resist, fibre-reactive dyed on cotton, 1998.

(Photo: Takashi Hatakegama)

DYES AND DYEING METHODS

Modern dye chemistry began in 1856 when William Henry Perkin was experimenting with the synthesis of quinine and aniline. By accident he isolated a black tar-like substance that he discovered contained a colour precipitate. Experimentation with this produced a purple aniline, referred to subsequently by the trade name mauvine (giving rise to the colour name mauve), and also by the nickname Perkin's purple. Owing to its amazing light- and wash-fastness, this coal-tar dye monopolized the dyer's art, despite being very expensive. Rapid experimentation produced brilliant colours, including magenta in 1859, aniline blue in 1860 and the first water-soluble dye in 1862. These synthetic dyes were a great advance on the longer and less predictable dye processes of natural dyestuffs and soon other classes of dye were discovered: direct dyes in 1884, and synthetic indigo and vat dyes in 1897 which were developed from Adolf von Baeyer's work on indigotin. Increasing demand for improved fastness prompted the invention of mordant dyes, including azoic dyes and their various adaptations, which were marketed in the early 20th century. In 1956, fibre-reactive dyes were developed and manufactured by Imperial Chemical Industries in the UK.

Today, petroleum rather than coal-tar is used as the basis for the synthetic dye industry. There are innumerable brand names on the market, but in fact the dyestuffs are actually produced by only a small number of companies.

DYES SUITABLE FOR BATIK

Dyestuffs suitable for making batik must be capable of being applied to natural fibres in cold water.

To the lay person, the chemistry may be somewhat formidable and the choice of dyestuffs perplexing, but with clear guidelines, colour mixing is made accessible and economical.

There are six categories of dyestuff suitable for batik:

- Fibre-reactive
- Naphthol and azoic
- Vat
- Direct
- Acid
- Basic

GENERAL DYE THEORY

Most organic fibrous matter absorbs water. If the water contains a colouring, either in a paste or liquid form, it will become attached to the fibre. The intensity of the colour increases as the dyeing process proceeds, transferring it until the dye bath is exhausted. To secure the colour and make it fast and evenly spread, compounds called assistants are used in the dye bath.

Liquid Ratio

To dye the cloth successfully, the whole cloth must be evenly exposed to the water containing the dye. The ratio indicates how much water is required for the dye bath. Most recipes call for a ratio of 30:1. It is important to note that this is not the ratio of water to dyestuff but of water to *cloth*, calculated by weight, so in this example there should be 30 times more water than the weight of cloth. (1 g of water has a volume of 1 ml and 1 oz of water has a volume of 1 fl oz.) 100 g cloth x 30 = 3000 g water (3 litres) or 1 3/4 oz cloth x 30 = 52 1/2 oz (52 1/2 fl oz).

Short dye baths (those which transmit their colour in the shortest amount of time) have a low ratio of water to cloth, perhaps as small as 5:1, which would give a high concentration of dye.

Percentage Calculation of Dye Solution

The strength of colour is determined by the ratio of the weight of dye to the weight of dry cloth. This percentage is important as it determines both the shade and the fastness of the dye bath. To assess the correct ratio, records of recipes can be kept to achieve accurate results.

A stock solution may make a 5 per cent shade. This would be calculated as follows:

Dyeing equipment: non-reactive bowls, spoons, baths, jugs etc.

- 50 g of dyestuff in 1000 ml (34 fl oz) water = 5 per cent colour shade
- 5 g (1/6 oz) in 1000 ml (34 fl oz) water = 0.5 per cent colour shade

- Generally, 5 per cent would be for a dark shade, whilst 0.5 per cent would be very pale.

FIBRE-REACTIVE DYES

Fibre-reactive dyes are the most effective and economical for batik. These were developed by ICI and offer the advantage of simple application by immersion or brush, combined with a greater degree of light- and washing-fastness. The brilliant range of colours achieve their fullest intensity on cellulose fibres (particularly mercerized cotton), but may also be used on silk and wool, though with less affinity and diminished absorption. The reaction is caused by the presence in the dye bath of an alkali (soda or washing soda) that bonds with the actual fibre (that is, the chemical composition of the fibre alters to form an inseparable compound with the dye). If the alkali is not present, then this action does not occur and the colour will wash out. Because the dye is reacting with the water as well as to the cellulose (a double decomposition process known as hydrolysis), the colour in the dye bath deteriorates, so it has an effective life of only about four hours. To ensure that the reaction between the dyestuffs and the fibre proceeds effectively, it is sufficient to air-dry the cloth for fixation to take place.

Proper control of the factors, together with attention to the rinsing and soaping treatments, will ensure fastness in the wet processes. The most popular dyes in this category are the Procion 'MX' series. The 'HE' series is not suitable as these dyes cannot be used cold.

1. Reduce dye powder to a smooth paste.

2. Add to bath, top up with cold water and stir.

3. Prepare salt, add to bath and stir.

4. Place fabric in dye and gently agitate.

5. After 15 minutes, remove fabric and add the alkali, soda.

6. Replace fabric, continue to turn regularly for another 45 minutes.

Hang on line to dry.

Procion 'M'X Reactive Dyes

Trade colour	Code	Actual Colour
Yellow	MX-8G	Brilliant Yellow
Yellow	MX-4G	Lemon
Yellow	MX-GR	Golden Yellow
Orange	MX-2R	Clear Orange
Scarlet	MX-G	Scarlet
Red	MX-5B	Brilliant Red
Red	MX-8B	Fuchsia
Rubine	MX-B	Rubine
Navy	MX-RB	Midnight Blue
Blue	MX-7RB	Ultramarine Violet
Blue	MX-2R	Royal Blue
Blue	MX-G	Cerulean
Turquoise	MX-G	Aquamarine Turquoise
Brown	MX-GRN	Rust
Brown	MX-3 RD	Burnt Umber
Olive	MX-3G	Olive Green

All the above have 3–4 per cent shade value, which generates the standard colour. By increasing the percentage the colour deepens. There is no black in the Procion range; it can be obtained by mixing three parts navy (MX-RB), one and a half parts yellow (MX-GR) and half part red (MX-5B). Kenactive, however, produce a ready-made black. The three primary

equivalent colours, red MX-8B, turquoise MX-G and yellow MX-8G, when mixed, give a full spectrum of colour.

Black may have to be applied several times to give good depth. An alternative is to use the mechanically-bonded naphthol dye for stronger overdyed colour with reactives as a base.

Chemicals

The following compounds are used in fibre-reactive dyeing:

Alkali the alkalis recommended for batik are anhydrous sodium carbonate (soda ash) and sodium bicarbonate. These are the essential fixing agents.

Common table salt this facilitates the penetration and even quality of dyeing and good colour yield.

Urea synthesized from natural gas, this is used as a solubilizing and hydroscopic agent. It helps the dyestuff dissolve more effectively and also delays the chemical reaction with the water by absorbing moisture from the atmosphere. Urea proves an effective ingredient when painting or spraying as it retards the fixing process.

Resist salt L a mild oxidizing agent which helps to increase colour yield.

Water softener a softener such as Calgon (sodium hexame taphosphate) neutralizes any metallic salts which might interfere with the dyeing process. Hard water can cause coagulation with some dyes and thickeners.

Bowls of dye

Pre-Treatment of Fabric

If the cloth has not been prepared for dyeing, it should be thoroughly machine washed in hot soapy water to remove any sizing or dressing that may prevent dye absorption. Rinsing and soaking in warm water with 2–4 g ($1/14$–$1/7$ oz) of a soap-free detergent – metapex or a wetting agent – will open the pores of the fabric. Excess water should be allowed to drip off before immersing in the bath.

Immersion Dyeing

For accurate results, the proportions of dyestuff, chemical, fabric and water must be measured, particularly when the exact shade has to be repeated. The dye bath recipe is as follows:

- Water = 30 x dry weight of cloth (as an example, 90 cm (1 yd) of fine cotton weighs 120 g / 4$1/4$ oz).
- Dyestuff: 0.5–4 g ($1/56$ –$1/7$ oz) dye to 1 litre (34 fl oz) dye liquid, depending on shade.
- Salt: for 2 g ($1/14$ oz) dye, 60 g (2$1/8$ oz) salt to 1 litre (34 fl oz) dye liquid; 80 g (2$4/5$ oz) salt for deeper shades.
- Soda ash: 10 g ($1/3$ oz) to 1 litre dye liquid; 20 g ($7/10$ oz) soda ash for deeper shades.

The procedure for dyeing is as follows:

1. Dissolve salt and soda in hot water (60° C / 140° F) in two separate containers (100 ml / 3^1/$_2$ fl oz imperial / 3 ^{2}/$_5$ fl oz US).

2. Reduce dye powder to a paste of smooth consistency using a small amount of warm water.

3. Add dye to dye bath and stir.

4. Immerse fabric and agitate to ensure thorough penetration.

5. Add salt solution in three equal portions over 15 minutes. Remove fabric for each addition.

6. Add soda solution to dye bath and stir.

7. Replace fabric for further 45 minutes, turning regularly.

8. Remove fabric.

9. Air-dry, preferably in humid atmosphere, for at least 2–3 hours.

10. After final dyeing, remove wax and rinse first in cold, then warm water until the water runs clear. Wash in hot water with a mild detergent soap.

Note that once the soda has been added to the dye bath the dye loses its effectiveness after a few hours. A shorter dyeing method is possible by adding the salt measure in one go and dyeing for less time. However, there is a greater tendency to blotching and streaking with this method. The shade of colour will also not be as deep. Handle the waxed fabric with great care in the bath to prevent unnecessary breaks in the resist.

Brushing dye colour into unwaxed areas of the cloth.

Fast Black K-Salt

The majority of reactive colours will react with this particular fast salt (diaza) in various shades of brown when overdyed, imitating the soga colour found in Javanese batik.

1. Dissolve 4–10 g ($^1/_7$–$^1/_3$ oz) fast black salt in warm water.
2. Add one litre of cold water.
3. Immerse dry fabric for about 5 minutes.
4. Rinse and soap.

Silk or Wool Dyeing

A very high degree of wet fastness is achieved by chemical linkage to the fibre. It is essential, therefore, that the silk is degummed before dyeing. On silk, the reactive dyes lose their effectiveness after three or four overdyeings, as the bonding sites on the fibre molecules become occupied by the dye already applied. A mechanically bonded vat or acid dye is worth considering as a final substantial colour.

The recipe and procedure followed is the same as that for cotton except that, when dyeing wool, both the salt and soda ash are replaced by acetic acid or white vinegar. The fabric must be well rinsed.

Brush Dye Application for Cotton and Silk

For painting, spraying, sponging or splashing techniques, fibre-reactive dyes are applied in a concentrated form. As they are applied directly and

Upstart Noel Dyrenforth

127 x 95 cm (50 x 37 ¹/₂ in).

Wax-resist, reactive dyed/sprayed and discharged on cotton, 1992.

not immersed in a bath, the fixation time has to be extended by the use of urea which helps to delay the dyeing process to allow reaction to occur.

First prepare a litre (34 fl oz) of chemical water which can be stored indefinitely at room temperature. Dissolve 4–5 g ($1/7$–$1/6$ oz) Calgon, 140 g ($4^{15}/_{16}$ oz) urea and 10 g ($1/3$ oz) resist salt L in 500 ml ($17^{1}/_{2}$ fl oz) hot water. Add cold water to make up 1 litre.

The dye recipe and procedure is as follows:

- Dyestuff: 0.25–3 g ($1/_{113}$–$1/9$ oz) dye (depending on colour strength) to 25 ml (1 fl oz) of chemical water.
- Soda ash: 1 g ($1/_{28}$ oz) soda ash, plus 0.25 g ($1/_{113}$ oz) soda bicarbonate, dissolved in a little warm water.

1. Make up dye powder paste in a little warm water to a strength according to the colour intensity required.
2. Add required amount of cold chemical water, approximately 50 ml (2 fl oz).
3. Add dissolved alkali (soda ash/bicarbonate) just before use.
4. Apply dye to fabric.
5. Air-dry for at least 12 hours.
6. Rinse out in running, soapy water.

Note that dry heat, ironing, or steaming can all improve fastness. Care should be taken not to overload colour so that the fabric surface becomes powdery.

A variation is to pre-treat the fabric by immersing it in a solution of soda ash (30 g / 1¹/₁₆ oz of soda ash to I litre / 34 fl oz of water) for about 10 mins, drying it, then painting on dye made up with 5 g (¹/₆ oz) urea to 100 ml (3¹/₂ fl oz imperial / 3²/₅ fl oz US) of water.

Thickening Dye for Direct Application

In certain instances it may be an advantage to control the spread of the dye solution by adding sodium alginate (which can be bought under the trade name Manutex). This is a powder that swells in water and does not react with the dyestuffs and may be removed finally by washing. The thickness is determined by the absorbency of the fabric and dyes used. A thinner solution can be used as a size. Store in an airtight container in the refrigerator. Procedure is as follows:

1. Sprinkle 4 g (¹/₇ oz) of sodium alginate to a litre of chemical water (recipe on page 82), or proportionately less, as it goes a long way.
2. Stir or mix with an electric blender for several minutes until it has formed an even consistency.
3. Leave to stand for at least an hour. Stir up before use.
4. Turn dye powder into a paste using thickened chemical water. Blend thoroughly.
5. Apply the dye and leave for at least 12 hours for fixation to occur.
6. Rinse cloth under cold running soapy water, increase temperature and finally soap and boil.

Direct application of dye colour with brush.

Fixation of Directly Applied Dyes

Although the natural drying process is perfectly adequate to fix the dye in the fibre, the presence of a warm humid atmosphere can speed up the process. In direct application, when the fabric has to air-dry for a long time, the presence of heat and moisture hastens the process. The fabric should first be allowed to dry by atmospheric steaming, pressure steaming or steam-baking in an oven, or by simply steam-ironing for five minutes. After fixing, the fabric should be rinsed in cold running water, ensuring that the material is open and the unfixed dye is washed out. After adding soap, the water temperature should be increased and the fabric boiled.

NAPHTHOL OR AZOIC DYES

These dyes produce extremely fast colours by the interaction of two dye baths. The first bath impregnates the cloth with a chemical and this, in turn, reacts with the dyestuff in the second bath to form an insoluble compound within the fibre. The process is instantaneous, unrivalled for its depth of colour and extremely fast to light, washing and boiling. The entire procedure can be completed in 15 minutes. Owing to their advantages and their similarity to indigo dyeing techniques, these dyes are the most frequently used in Indonesia. Used originally on cellulose fibres, they give good but somewhat different results on silk and wool. The dye bath is active for approximately six hours, providing it is kept out of direct light. Owing to the instantaneous colour response, it is

Linked Layers Tony Dyer

213 x 41 cm (84 x 16 in).

Wax-resist, azoic dyed silk, handmade felt,

machine-stitched, 2001.

particularly important to remove all size, starch or processing oils from the fabric before dyeing.

At least two of each piece of equipment is needed and only non-reactive materials such as plastic, glass, stainless steel or enamel should be used. Small amounts of dye are used in relation to the weight of the fabric. Flat, wide baths are more practical for immersion methods. Measuring ingredients by volume (such as with a tea spoon) would give a distorted impression because the diazo salts weigh about twice as much as the naphthol per unit volume; it is therefore essential to measure by weight.

Chemicals

Caustic soda (sodium hydroxide) solution is the only chemical required for naphthol dyeing. The solution is prepared by dissolving 441 g (15½ oz) caustic soda in 1 litre of cold water. The caustic soda should be carefully added, stirring all the time and ensuring that splashes are avoided as the solution releases heat and is dangerous. After allowing it to cool it should be placed in a dark bottle and closed with either a plastic or cork stopper. The bottle should be clearly labelled and stored in a safe place, out of reach of children. If the solution comes into contact with the skin, it must be washed immediately in water. The amount of caustic soda used in the dye bath is, however, fractional and the danger negligible.

A small amount of methylated spirit helps to dissolve the naphthol to a paste and acts as a wetting agent.

Drawing in wax on silk.

Dye Recipe

The standard proportion by weight of naphthol to diazo salts per litre is:

- Bath 1: 2 g ($^1/_{14}$ oz) naphthol to 1 litre (34 fl oz) of water
- Bath 2: 4 g ($^1/_7$ oz) diazo salts to 1 litre of water

This will give a medium-strength colour. For a lighter shade, put 1 g ($^1/_{28}$ oz) naphthol in 1 litre of water in bath 1, followed by 2 g diazo salts in 1 litre of water in bath 2. For a darker shade, put 2 g naphthol in 1 litre of water in bath 1, followed by 6 g ($^1/_5$ oz) diazo salts in 1 litre of water in bath 2.

A coded range of naphthol and a wide range of colour salts is commercially available. By using the same base with a variety of colour salts or different bases with one colour salt, a vast range of colours can be achieved. It is sufficient, however, to begin with just two or three of each. Individual recipes and preferences will result from experimentation.

Preparation of Naphthol Bath

1. Make a paste from 2 g naphthol with a touch of methylated spirit in a measuring cup and work to a smooth consistency.
2. Add 25 ml (1 fl oz) of boiling water and stir the solution, making certain the chemical has completely dissolved.
3. Immediately add 5 to 20 ml ($^1/_6$ to $^2/_3$ fl oz) caustic soda solution (see *Chemicals* opposite). Stir as solution is added drop by drop until the naphthol becomes clear and yellow, but use no more than is absolutely necessary.

4. Leave the solution to cool for a few minutes.

5. Add cold water to make the mixture up to 1 litre.

Note that if the naphthol does not clear when the caustic solution is added, it should be reheated to boiling point and stirred again.

Preparation of Diazo Salt Bath

1. Measure out 4 g ($^1/_7$ oz) diazo salt.

2. Mix to a paste with cold water.

3. Add cold water to make up to 1 litre (34 fl oz).

Procedure for Dyeing

1. Place the wet fabric in the naphthol bath. It is essential that the whole fabric is impregnated for about 5 minutes.

2. Lift out and allow all the excess naphthol to drip back into the bath. Hang for at least 10 minutes – longer for heavier fabric.

3. Submerge the fabric in the diazo salt bath. The colour will develop immediately on contact. Agitate the fabric and leave for 5 minutes or until there is no further colour change. Too rapid removal will result in a loss of rub-fastness. Hang out until it is drip free.

4. Rinse in running cold water until clear.

5. Soap and boil the fabric to eliminate excess dye and to stabilize the colour.

Make sure you keep the two dye baths well apart. An excess of naphthol in the diazo salt bath exhausts the colour. In order to increase colour intensity, repeat this process, rinsing off each time after the second bath.

After removing the fabric from the naphthol bath, a quick rinse in a salt bath (50 g / 1³/₄ oz salt to 1 litre of cold water) will remove the excess naphthol and facilitate the dyeing process. This, however, is optional.

Direct Application by Brushing

Both naphthol and colour salts can be applied manually by brush or spray techniques. A thickener can be used for painting. This application offers considerable freedom, owing to the highly sensitive reaction between naphthol and colour salts in combination. Because the dyeing process involves two stages, how accurately one predicts the finished colour depends very much on experience.

When painting on the naphthol, the use of a fine natural bristle or hair brush is not recommended as the soda content will corrode it.

Colour Mixing

Naphthols have a colour spectrum ranging from intense black to subtle hues, all dependent on the proportion of naphthol to diazo salt in equal amounts of water. Shades can be produced by varying the proportion of naphthol to diazo salt. Never mix the two together. For a general indication of colour, note the following essential naphthols and their coding:

Waxing with fine pointed brush.

Naphthol AS/AS D	develops as colour of salt
Naphthol LB	develops brown values
Naphthol G	develops yellow values
Naphthol TR	develops pastel colours
Naphthol BO	develops strong colour values
Naphthol GR	develops green with blue salts

Naphthol BS, SR, OL all vary slightly. The strongest salts are Red B, Blue BB, Black K, BTL and ANS. Other colours are: Scarlet GG, Blue B, Violet B, Bordeaux GP, Orange RD, Green BB, Yellow GC.

To mix these colours, generally use a proportion of 2 g naphthol to 4 g colour salt to a litre of water (lighter shades would be obtained from proportions of 0.5 g to 1 g to 1 litre; for darker shades use considerably more – only by testing with different proportions will you get the benefit of the full range of colour). As an example, if you use naphthol G with Red B diazo salts, you develop a golden yellow. Used with LB, the same salt gives a red-brown.

AS BO + Scarlet GG develops clear red
AS BO + Red B develops maroon
AS G + Blue BB develops ochre
AS G + Red B develops golden yellow
AS LB + Yellow GC develops pale brown
AS LB + Red B develops red-brown

AS + Blue BB develops royal blue

AS + Red B develops light crimson

A deep black develops if you increase the proportion to 2:8 using AS BO and Black ANS. Re-dip if necessary to increase depth.

It is also possible to mix the naphthols themselves; for example, for brown mix $^1/_2$ g AS D with $1^1/_2$ g AS G using blue BB.

On silk similar colours can be obtained by the use of vinegar or acetic acid in the diazo salt bath. Use approximately 2 ml to 1 litre of water.

VAT DYES

These are unique in that they are insoluble in water and have no affinity with the fibre until they are reduced to a soluble form by an alkali solution. They are used primarily on cotton, although they can be used on silk and are extremely fast to light and washing – in fact more fast than any other type. The dye will appear colourless until exposed to oxidizing agents which develop the colour. The shade is determined by how often and how long the cloth is dipped in the indigo bath.

The most significant in this class is synthetic indigo. It was first manufactured in 1897 and has generally replaced the natural form. The dyeing procedures are direct and absorbing; the development of the colour is fascinating. It is important to handle the cloth carefully during dyeing to ensure that the wax does not break down. The vat has to remain at a temperature of at least 20° C (68° F) to be effective.

Recipe and Procedure

30 g (1^1/$_{16}$ oz) indigo vat 60 per cent grains

30 g (1^1/$_{16}$ oz) caustic soda (100 per cent)

20 g (^{7}/$_{10}$ oz) sodium hydrosulphite

10 litres (340 fl oz) water

Please note that caustic soda and sodium hydrosulphite are corrosive chemicals that will cause burns to the eyes and skin. Especially rigorous safety precautions need to be taken to avoid skin and eye contact. Safety spectacles, heavy-duty rubber gloves, dust mask and protective clothing must be worn.

The procedure for dyeing is as follows:

1. Measure out 10 litres of warm water (25° C/ 77° F) into a large plastic vat.
2. Carefully add the caustic soda to a ^{1}/$_2$ litre of cold water (*not* water to caustic soda).
3. Add this solution to the vat. Stir gently.
4. Sprinkle the sodium hydrosulphite slowly onto the surface of the liquid in the vat and stir to ensure even dispersal of the powder.
5. Add the indigo powder or grains to the vat, stirring gently to discourage air bubbles, which would weaken the mixture.
6. After about 10 minutes, a brilliant purple sheen will have formed on the surface.

Iowa Amri Yahya

400 x 140 cm (157 x 55 in), detail.

Indigosol dyed on cotton, 1986.

7. Cover with blanket and leave to stand for one hour to fully reduce the indigo.

8. Wet cloth and gently wring it out before submerging into the dye vat. Avoid trapping air pockets.

9. Agitate the cloth under the surface to ensure the entire surface is exposed; leave in for about 5 minutes.

10. Withdraw dyed cloth without allowing it, as far as possible, to drip back into vat. Since the solution will start to oxidize as soon as it makes contact with the air, drops of oxidized dye falling back into the vat will weaken the remaining solution, reducing its effectiveness in later dippings.

11. Quickly open out cloth and hang on line to oxidize evenly for about 5 minutes.

12. Rinse in cold water until clear.

The colour can be intensified by repeat dipping until the necessary strength is achieved. The vat dye can be used until exhausted. Ensure that the vat is kept covered when not in use. The strength can be revived by simply adding half of the original quantities of each of the chemical components.

Adopt care when handling the wax-resist fabric during immersion dyeing. As the vat liquid remains at about 20° C (68° F), the micro crystalline wax or beeswax content in the resist should be increased at the outset to strengthen and withstand the temperature.

Direct or Application Dyes

These dyestuffs have an affinity with cellulose fibres and can be used on silk. They work best in a dye bath of 85–90° C (185–194° F), but have to be cooled for use in batik. They are so named because they do not need a mordant and are easy to apply. They are not very wash-fast, but this can be improved by after-treatment with recommended fixatives. The most common brand, Deka L, is a union of the direct and acid components.

These dyes are soluble in water and can be freely mixed. They possess the advantage of having a brilliant range of colours including a good black with an unlimited array of hues. They are excellent for discharge, and once used, can be stored and reused.

The procedure for using them is as follows:

1. Make a paste mixing 10–20 g ($1/_3$–$7/_{10}$ oz) with warm water.

2. Add 1 litre (34 fl oz) of water and bring to the boil.

3. Dissolve ten times the amount of salt to dye powder.

4. Add to the dye bath.

5. Leave the solution to cool.

6. Immerse the fabric for 30–45 minutes.

7. Rinse fabric.

Brushing and blending dye colour on silk.

For dyeing silk or wool, replace salt with white vinegar or acetic acid. Steaming is generally required to fix the colour.

ACID DYES

These dyestuffs have a direct affinity with protein fibres such as silk or wool. They are economical to use and have a range of vibrant colours although they are not wash-fast. They should always be dry-cleaned.

Specific dye ranges for hand-painting are made from mixtures of acid dyes by manufacturers such as Jacquard, Sennelier and Dupont.

Acids are used as dyeing assistants. For the craft dyer, acetic acid or white vinegar is recommended, although using ammonium sulphate as an acid donor is more of a guarantee against streaking as it slows the dyeing process. Pre-metalized dyestuffs (which are similar to acid) yield intense colour and are exceptionally resistant to fading. Both types of dyes require steaming or colour fixation.

The dyeing procedure is similar to that applying to direct dyes, but acetic acid or Glauber's salt is used in the process.

BASIC DYES

This group comprises a number of dyes that can be applied to silk and wool. A mordant is needed for cotton. These basic dyes were the first synthetic dyes made from coal-tar derivatives. They have an organic colour base soluble in an acid solution. They produce bright colours but have poor fastness and are rarely used in industrial dyeing today. However, they are economical and easy to use for the craft dyer. Their wash-fastness can be improved with treatment in tannic acid, although this has the effect of subduing the colour. The fabric should be dry-cleaned.

The procedure for using basic dyes is as follows:

1. Make a paste with 0.5–1 g ($^1/_{56}$–$^1/_{28}$ oz) dyestuff to 1 teaspoon of acetic acid (or manufacturer's fixative).

2. Add 250 ml (9 fl oz imperial, 8$^1/_8$ fl oz US) of hot water and stir.

3. Top up with 750 ml (25$^1/_2$ fl oz) of tepid water.

4. Immerse the fabric for 30–40 minutes.

5. Rinse the fabric.

DISCHARGE DYEING OR BLEACHING

Discharging is a chemical process to remove colour from a previously dyed fabric. This method of removing colour from the unwaxed areas offers a radical opportunity to reappraise and change colours while the work is in progress. All dyes are dischargeable to a lesser or greater extent depending on the strength of the chemicals used. However, because of their fastness, some reactive and naphthol colours are more resistant. Household bleach can be used on cotton, providing it is sufficiently diluted to ensure that the chlorine does not destroy the fibres. Bleach should be diluted from 3–10 times with cold water, depending on the shade required. The mix should be tested before immersing the actual work. On placing the fabric in the bath, it should be agitated for about 10 minutes to ensure complete evenness. The fabric is rinsed thoroughly afterwards with a subsequent washing in soapy water. For accelerated results, undiluted bleach can be applied with a brush. However, because

Discharge dyeing on paper.

A Place To Be Hetty van Boekhout

50 x 50 cm (19 $^2/_3$ x 19 $^2/_3$ in).

Wax-resist, reactive/discharged dyed paper, 2002.

of the intense action of the chlorine, it is essential to rinse the fabric to neutralize it before the fibres get damaged.

Remember that bleach is extremely dangerous. Wear rubber gloves, washing them in water after each procedure. Avoid inhaling fumes by working in a well-ventilated space and wearing a mask. If any chemicals touch the skin, wash immediately in plenty of running water. Protect the eyes by wearing safety goggles and ensure that rubber gloves are strong and not porous or damaged.

FIXING METHODS

Steaming

The procedure varies according to the dye used. With naphthol, reactive and vat-dyed fabrics, steaming is generally not required. With direct and acid dyes steaming is usually necessary. A number of liquid and powdered fixers are sometimes recommended by the manufacturers.

During steaming, heat and moisture combine to promote a permanent bond between the dye and the fibre. Reactive dye needs only 5–15 minutes. Acid or direct dyes require 60 minutes. These times depend on the amount of steam generated. Before proceeding, loose wax should be broken off and ironed out between absorbent paper. Paste or gutta evaporates during the steaming process.

Improvized vessels large enough to contain the wrapped fabric can be prepared as follows:

1. Set a wire rack 10 cm (4 in) high on the bottom of the container.
2. Fill with water to below platform level.
3. Place a layer of newspaper or cloth on the rack.
4. Boil the water.
5. Place unprinted paper or lining paper on the fabric back and front, fold it concertina-style or coil and tie it with string. Keep away from the side of the container.
6. Place wrapped fabric on platform and cover with a pad of newspaper or cloth to protect the fabric from condensation, or suspend the bundle from a stick placed across the top of the container.
7. Place a thick pad over the opening and put the lid on. Weight the lid down to build up the pressure, but not so tight that it prevents the steam from escaping.
8. Bring the water to the boil and steam for the recommended time, depending on the size and weight of the fabric. Add more water if it evaporates, since it is the balance between moisture and heat that is important.
9. Remove the fabric and untie it making sure none of the condensation falls on the fabric.

Professional bullet steamers with a capacity of up to 10 m (33 ft) of medium-weight fabric are available for small-scale production. They consist of a double-walled stainless steel tube placed in a hot water container. The fabric is rolled around an alloy bar with paper encasing it.

Other Fixing Methods

- Ironing with a warm steam iron.
- Air-drying in a warm, humid atmosphere for a day. Under the right conditions the dye will set. If it is too moist, the colour will run. If too dry, the powder will remain on the surface without penetrating and will partly wash out in the rinsing.
- Dry-bake wrapped in oven for 5 minutes at 141° C (285° F).

Finishing

The fabric should now be rinsed and agitated in running water so that any excess dye or chemical is washed away and does not stain the fabric. It should then be soaped out in a large bath with warm water. This process is vital to the handling and pliability of the fabric. In drying the fabric, wringing or twisting to remove the moisture should be avoided. While still damp, it can be finished by ironing to remove any stubborn creases.

Some dyes can be made more colourfast by a prescribed fixative, particularly for acid or direct dyes.

Application of dye with brush.

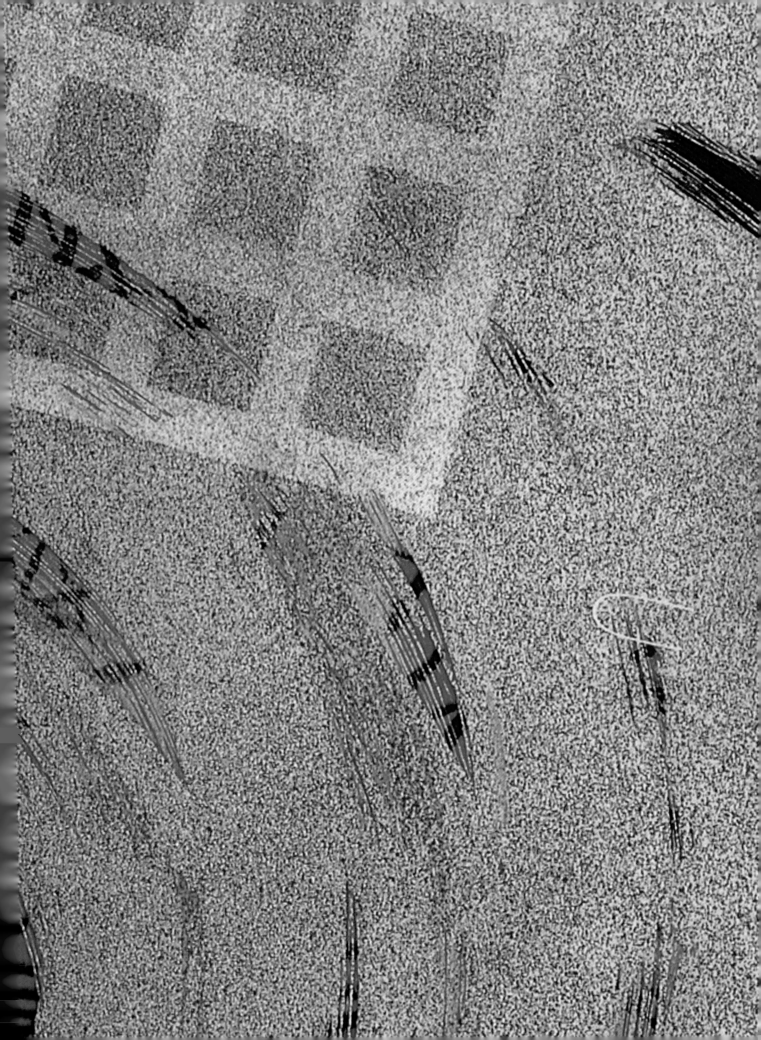

TECHNIQUES STEP-BY-STEP

THE ESSENCE OF BATIK

1 Heat the wax in a thermostatic pot (remember that the fluidity of the wax is controlled by its temperature and composition). Soften the brushes before using them by placing them in the wax for a few minutes.

2 Tightly stretch the cloth over a frame with pins. Load the bristle brush with a measured amount of wax, wipe off excess and apply to the cloth.

3 Experience the immediacy of the cloth being saturated by the dye. Equally powerful is the reaction of the wax-resist, repelling the colour. This response encapsulates the principle of the wax-resist dyed process.

4 Dry the cloth before subsequent application of wax.

The final colour pulls together the successive
wax and dye layers. 5

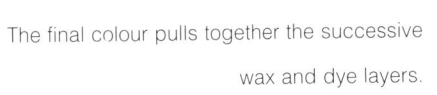

Clean excess dye from wax surface. 6

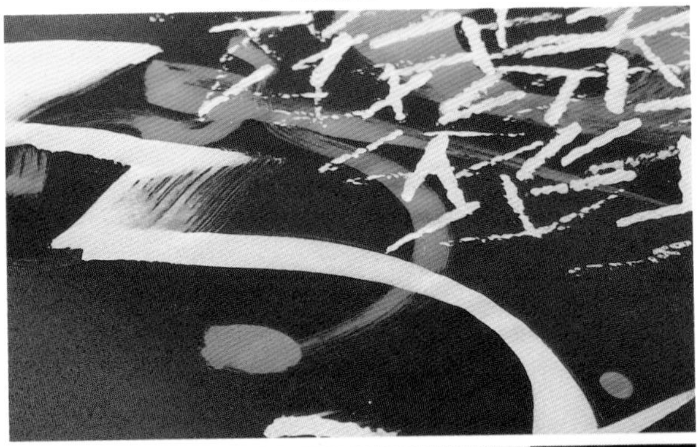

Press out wax with hot iron, absorbing it
between newsprint. Release from underlay.
Dry-clean or boil out remainder of wax to
restore fabric to its natural texture. 7

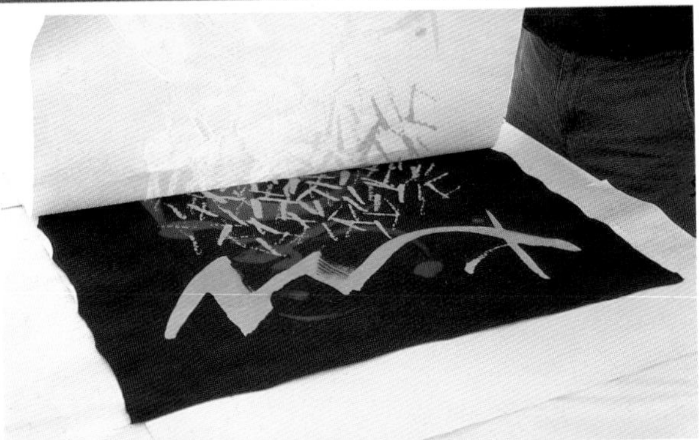

Remove excess dye by washing under cold
running water, then soak cloth in soapy warm
water. Dry and iron to complete process. 8

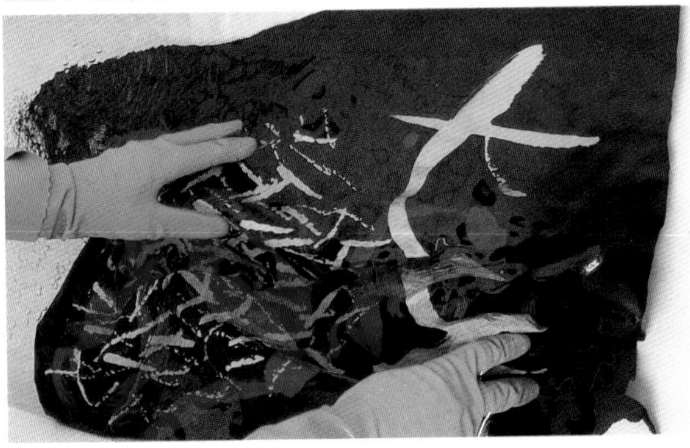

WORKING ON SILK

1 Fill canting three-quarters full with hot wax.

2 Clean outer surface of canting. Check working posture and access to tools and materials. Take a relaxed hold on the canting and stabilize (control by placing a finger on the work surface). Raise the spout of the canting slightly above the fabric to allow a free flow of wax.

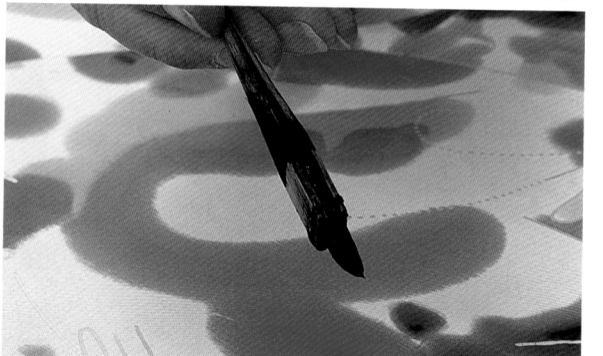

3 Apply the colour playfully, with a soft natural hair brush.

4 Permit dye to bleed and mix. Add water to loosen the colour.

First waxing on a multicoloured ground. 5

Background colour unifies the forms outlined by the wax. 6

Controlled wax lines lace the solid forms together. 7

Create added texture by padding hot wax on to the silk. 8

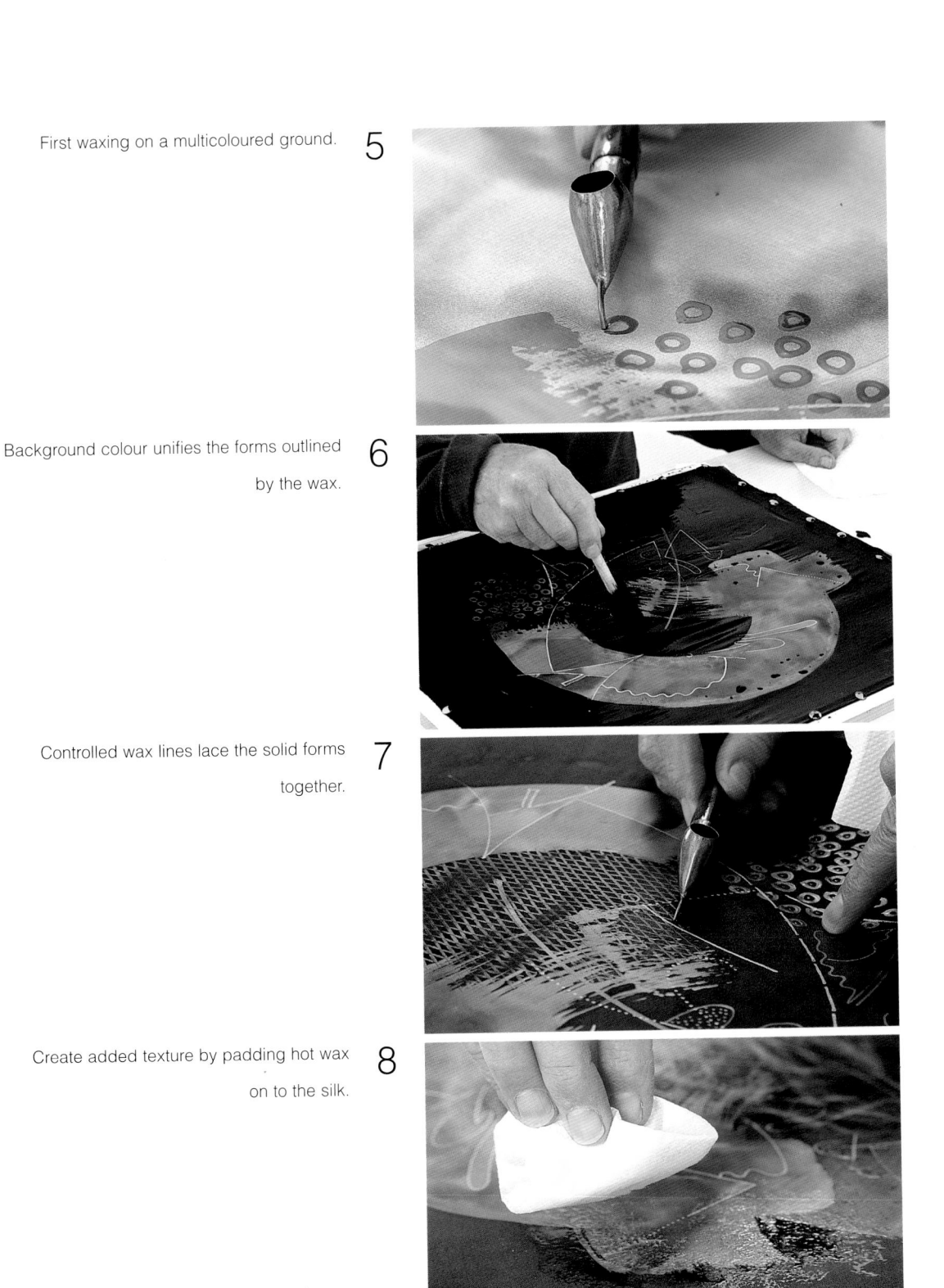

9 Brush on bleach till the unwaxed areas disintegrate. Rinse thoroughly, dry, and remove wax, partially by ironing. It is practical to leave a residue of wax in as the work is too fragile to clean.

10 Finished work.

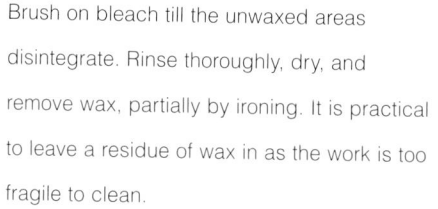

OUTLINE TECHNIQUE ON SILK

Fill canting with hot wax. Clean outer surface of canting.

1

Draw shapes on the cloth by a wax outline, rather than filling the shape. Check the line to ensure it is continuous and penetrates through the silk.

2

Brush on colour, using fine-hair brushes so that the silk draws on the dye instantly. Use a modest amount of dye relative to the area to be covered. Work quickly, overlapping for evenness.

3

By creating self-contained barriers of wax, a multicoloured batik can be planned in one waxing. Further waxings or the addition of salt crystals will add additional texture and interest.

4

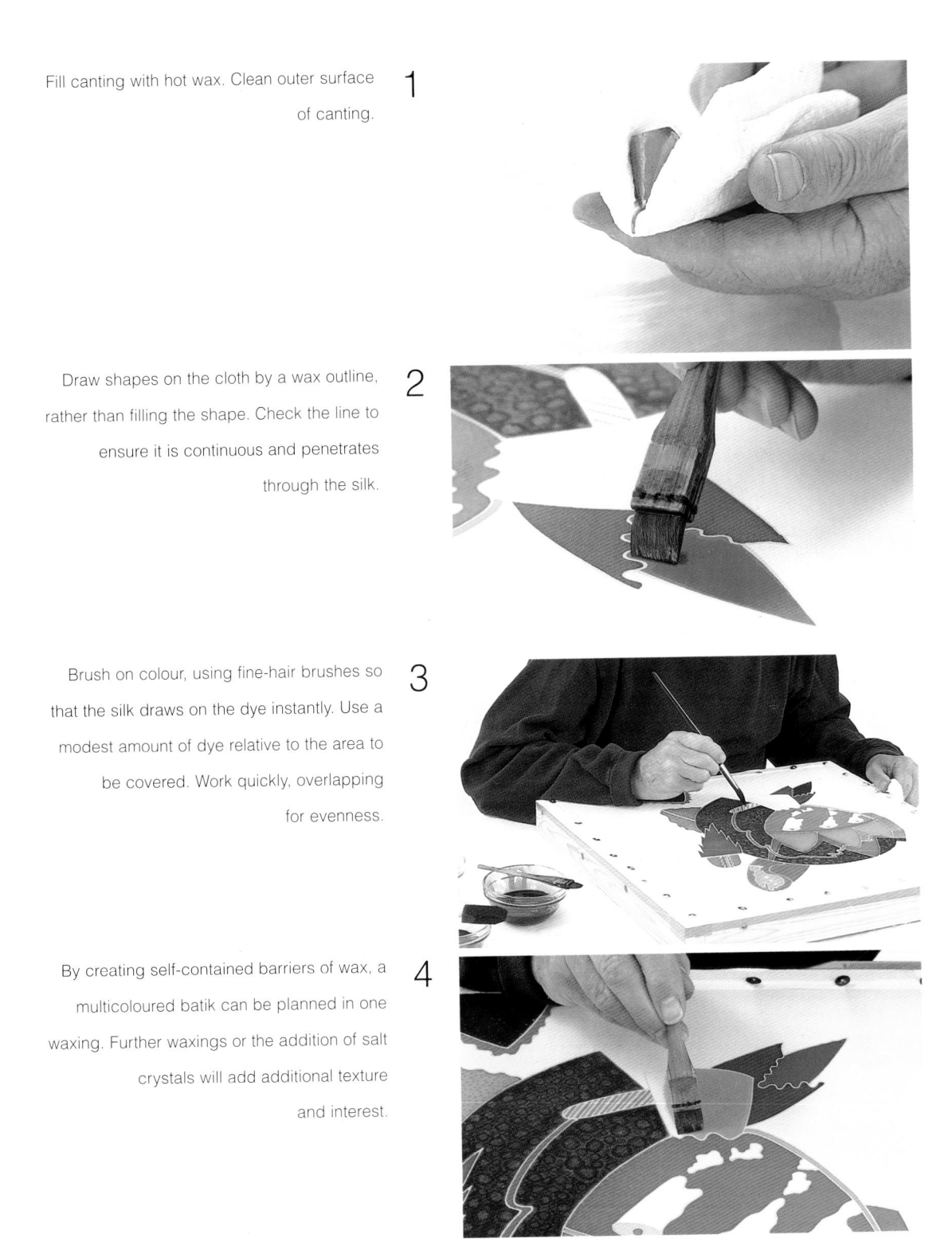

5   Finished work.

ETCHING OR SCRAFFITO IN WAX

Draw or trace the design onto the fabric. Brush an even amount of wax over the work area.

1

Place the waxed fabric onto a hard plastic or glass surface. Using a tool with a dull metal point so as not to damage the fabric, inscribe firmly into the wax surface, following the pencil lines. Textural interest can be added by cracking the wax.

2

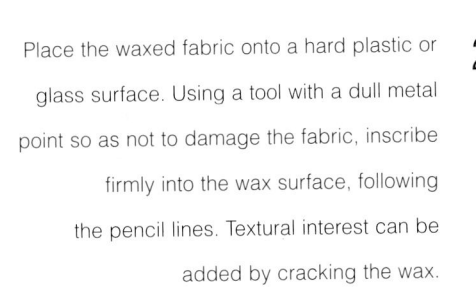

The etched line exposes the cloth to the action of the dye in the bath. Brushing will help penetration.

3

After dip dyeing, the surface is cleaned. The line revealed can be as refined and fresh as the serpentine line of a Picasso drawing.

4

5 Finished work.

DISCHARGE DYEING OR BLEACHING

The design in white chalk is clearly visible against the deep blue dyed ground. The background is reserved with wax. Refill the brush regularly for even penetration of hot wax into the fabric. Check back of cloth to ensure complete wax coverage.

1

The internal forms are dissected by regular wax lines.

2

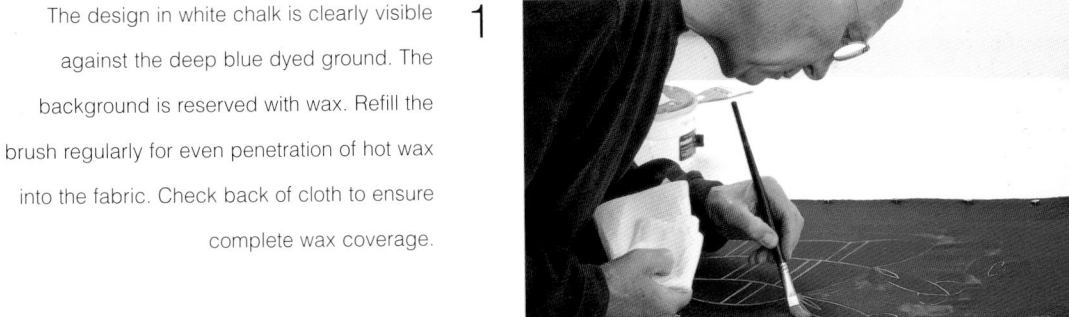

Having reserved the blue background, the unwaxed areas are subjected to the discharge solution to remove the colour.

3

When the bleach has taken effect, wash out immediately and thoroughly with cold water to stop the invasive action of the chlorine.

4

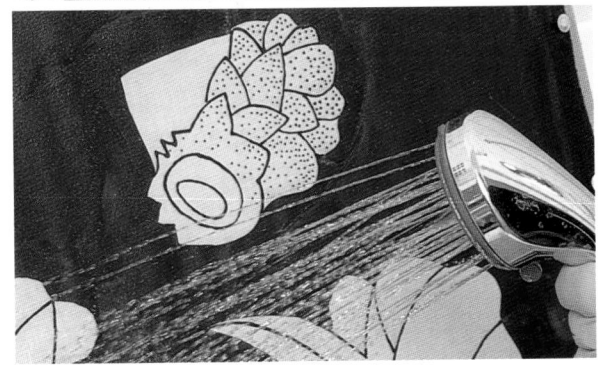

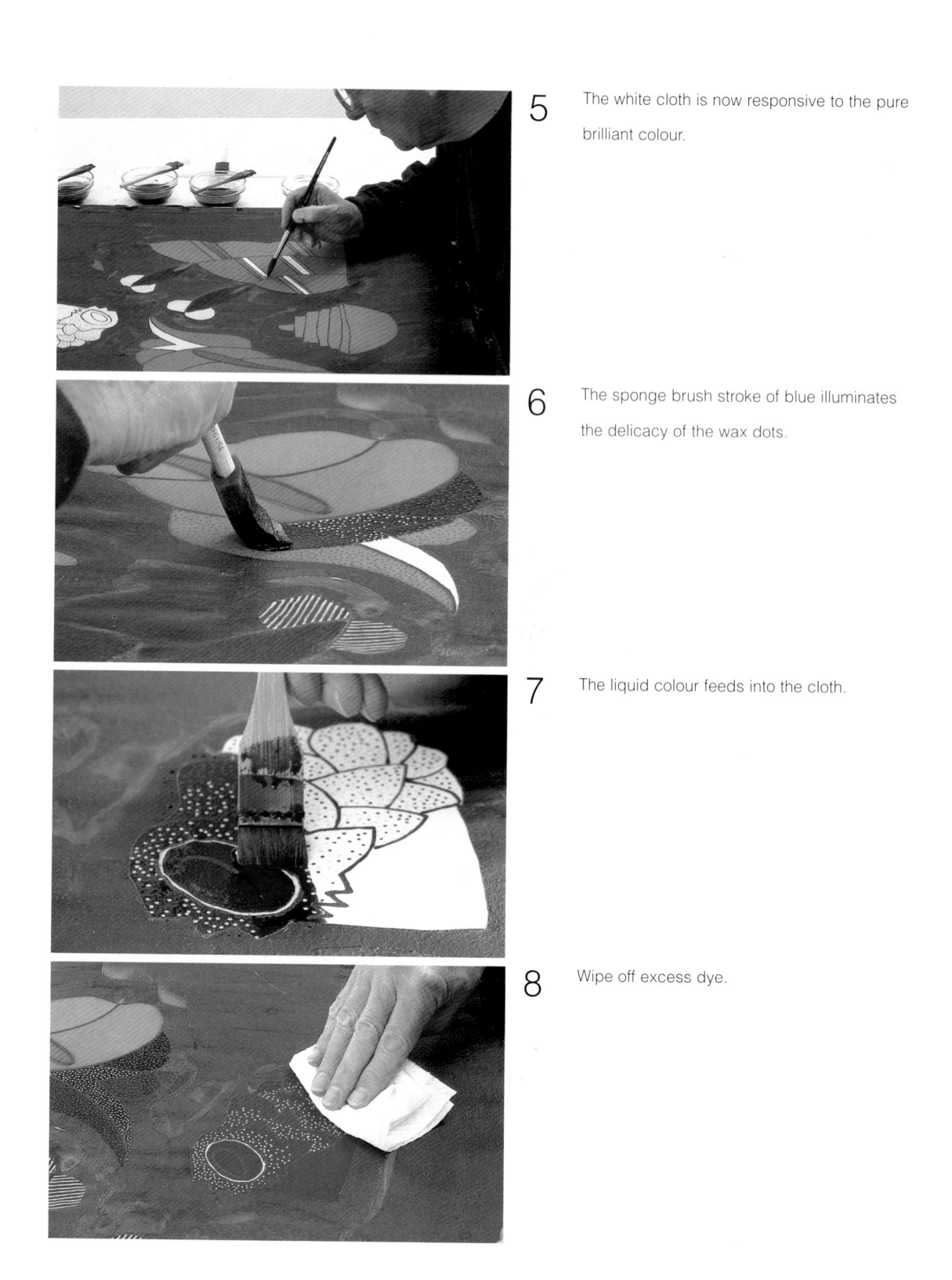

5 The white cloth is now responsive to the pure brilliant colour.

6 The sponge brush stroke of blue illuminates the delicacy of the wax dots.

7 The liquid colour feeds into the cloth.

8 Wipe off excess dye.

9 Finished work.

SPLATTER WAX WITH SHADED BACKGROUND

1 A shaded ground is a graduated wash of one or more colours. Prepare a number of tints or tones, and apply the lightest first, filling the brush sparingly. Use sweeping, overlapping strokes to produce an even ground.

2 Allow the dye to settle and partially dry. Brush on the deeper tone in the same manner as before. The dye will migrate if the frame is not flat or the fabric too wet. Use a clean, dry, soft brush to feather the edge. Rub and blend in the colour with a circular motion.

3 Apply the deeper red, following the same shading procedure as above.

4 The shading gives an accent and dimension to the fabric; the white a brilliance of light. Masking tape or stencils are cut and arranged on the cloth.

Dip a short bristle brush into the hot wax to soften. 5

By tapping the brush on a length of dowelling, a fine splatter of wax is rendered on the cloth. 6

Remove the masking tape. 7

Brush an orange dye over the whole waxed cloth; both the unwaxed structured form and the pointillistic effect of the wax are revealed, subtly juxtaposed. 8

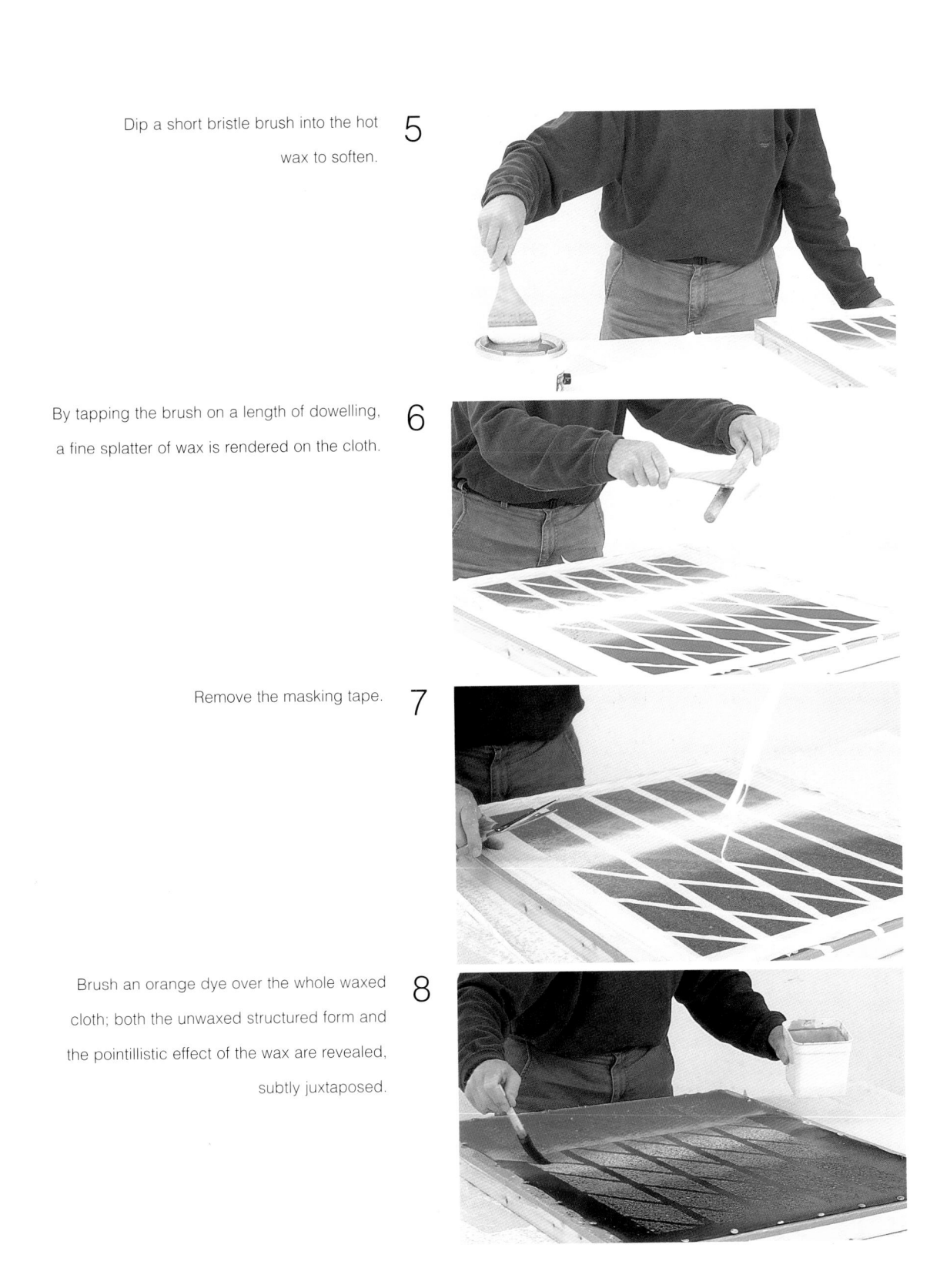

9 The delicate pattern of wax captures the undulating ground colour of the cloth.

10 Finished work.

WAX PRINTING

Providing that the stamp is made of a material which is both absorbent and a conductor of heat, a range of pattern blocks can be made out of metal strips, sponges, wood, felt, cardboard and so on.

1

An electric frying pan, with a sponge base in a shallow amount of wax, is ideal for this purpose. By varying the strength of the resist, the impressions can range from subtle to distinct.

2

Lay the fabric on to a plastic sheet with a soft underlay. Place the paper into the wax, release and dab off excess wax before printing firmly onto the material. Register the pattern and release. Refuel with wax and repeat procedure.

3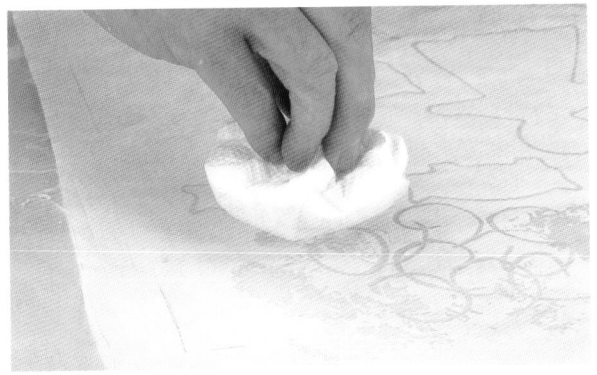

Brush over with dye colour. Besides being economical, this method of repeat patterning can result in interestingly complex designs.

4

WORKING ON PAPER

1 Lay tissue paper on newsprint for support and apply first waxing to reserve turquoise ground colour.

2 Brush over with dark blue and dry.

3 Brush wax with stabbing motion.

4 After bleaching back.

Iron off wax and remove top paper. Place newsprint on surface and iron out wax.

5

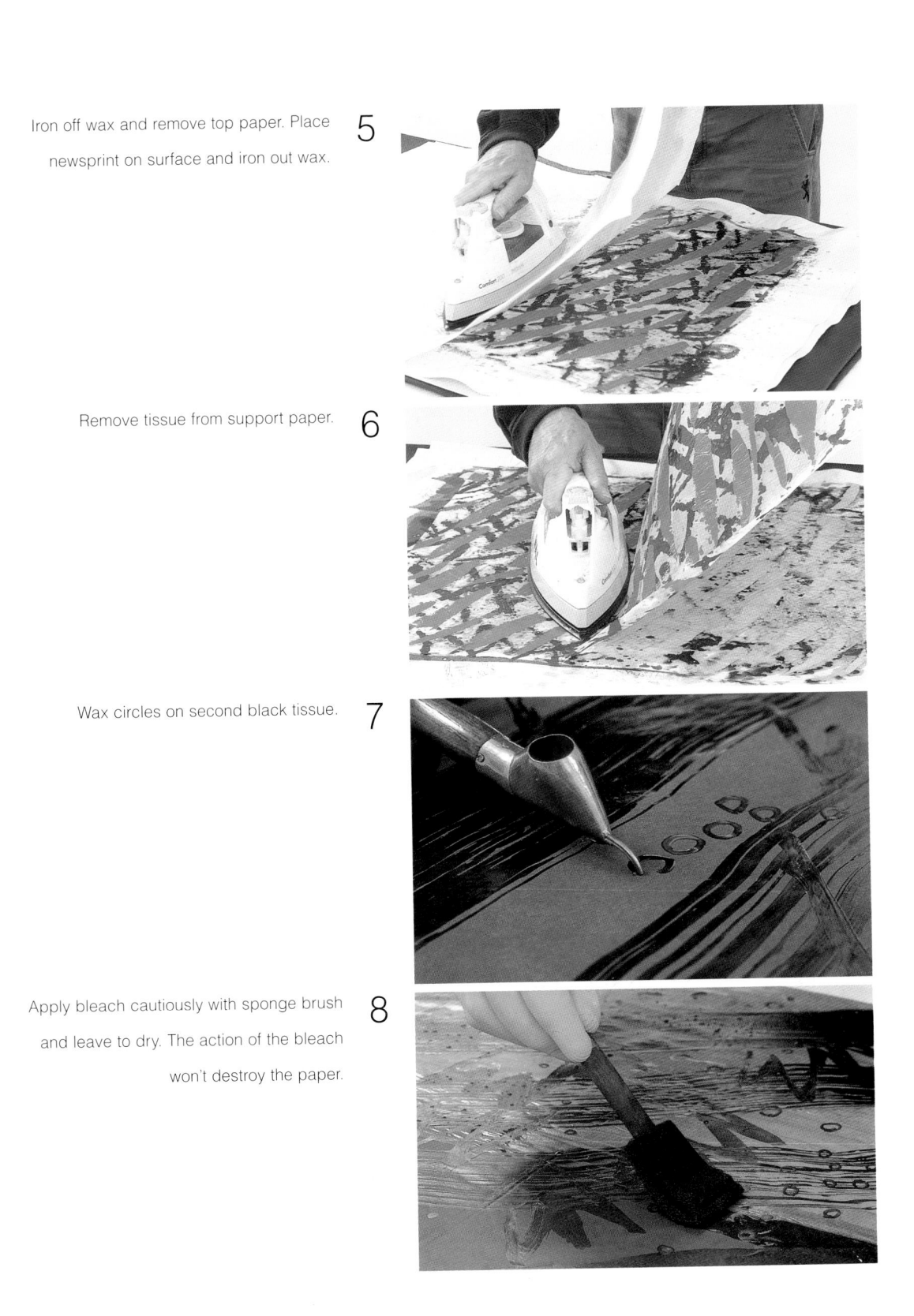

Remove tissue from support paper.

6

Wax circles on second black tissue.

7

Apply bleach cautiously with sponge brush and leave to dry. The action of the bleach won't destroy the paper.

8

9 After a further waxing and brushing on of the red colour, release tissue from base by ironing.

10 By using a soft-tipped brush, an expressive, rigorous wax line is formed on the paper. The tactile use of the brush enlivens the spirit of the line.

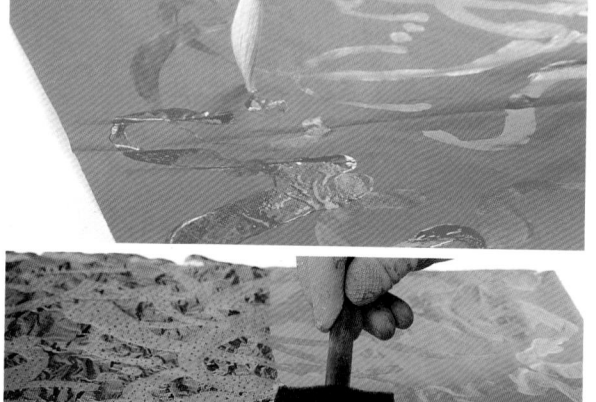

11 The colour fills the unprotected areas, enhancing the wax imagery.

12 Freely tearing and cutting the three papers, reassembling, layering, and combining pattern with transparency to form a collage.

Fusing the tissue paper together with wax and sealing it with a hot iron. **13**

Finished work. **14**

INTEGRATING TECHNIQUES

1 Securing masking tape to the white cloth in the form of a grid.

2 For protection, wear a mask and rubber gloves. Spray dye with an aerosol. The effect is misty, soft and spacious. Care must be taken not to over-spray, as this would undermine the stencil and make the colour too dense.

3 Remove tape after leaving cloth to dry for a few hours. The grid is the springboard for the whole composition.

4 Brush wax to protect the background, leaving the forms open for change.

The waxing process is a blending of technical prowess and sensitivity to the innate nature of the material.

5

The brushing of the dye colour emphasizes the subtle resistant powers of the wax and its characteristic vulnerability to the dye's invasive qualities.

6

The cone and cross images have both been bleached back to white. The deep blue swirl has first been partially waxed, then subsequently bleached.

7

To exploit your skill in drawing the wax line, try developing a personalized language of hieroglyphs.

8

9   The dye challenges the stubborn nature of the wax.

10   Turquoise filters into the expressively brushed wax, emphasizing and liberating the shapes and movement.

11   Filling in colour, restrained by the sharp edge of the wax.

12   The joy of the defining colour, the culmination of compounding wax and dye. As the process evolves, it becomes more intimate and enriching.

Finished work. 13

BOILING OUT WAX AND REWAXING

1   Canting resting in wax.

2   The wax line flows precisely from the canting's spout. A slight angle to the tool evens the flow. The hand can rest on the surface of the cloth for stability. Check your posture to ensure an uninhibited flow of energy through the arm. The vigour this imparts to the process will be visible in the final work.

3   Apply colour in bold curving strokes, bringing an undulation of light and dark blue to the background.

4   After drying, echo the same rhythm in wax; brush on both sides of the cloth. By overlaying the wax, the effect of the brushing is variable. Some areas will be totally resistant to the dye whilst others may be fragile and break down.

The areas of wax that remain open will respond and absorb the black dye. Note that it is brushed vigorously on to both sides of the cloth or, alternatively, dipped into a dye bath.

5

The waxed cloth is submerged into the boiling water. A small amount of soda ash helps to eject the wax from the cloth. Rapidly stir the cloth, and scoop it out after a few minutes.

6

Plunge the cloth directly into a bucket of cold water which will solidify any remaining wax.

7

Hang up to dry.

8

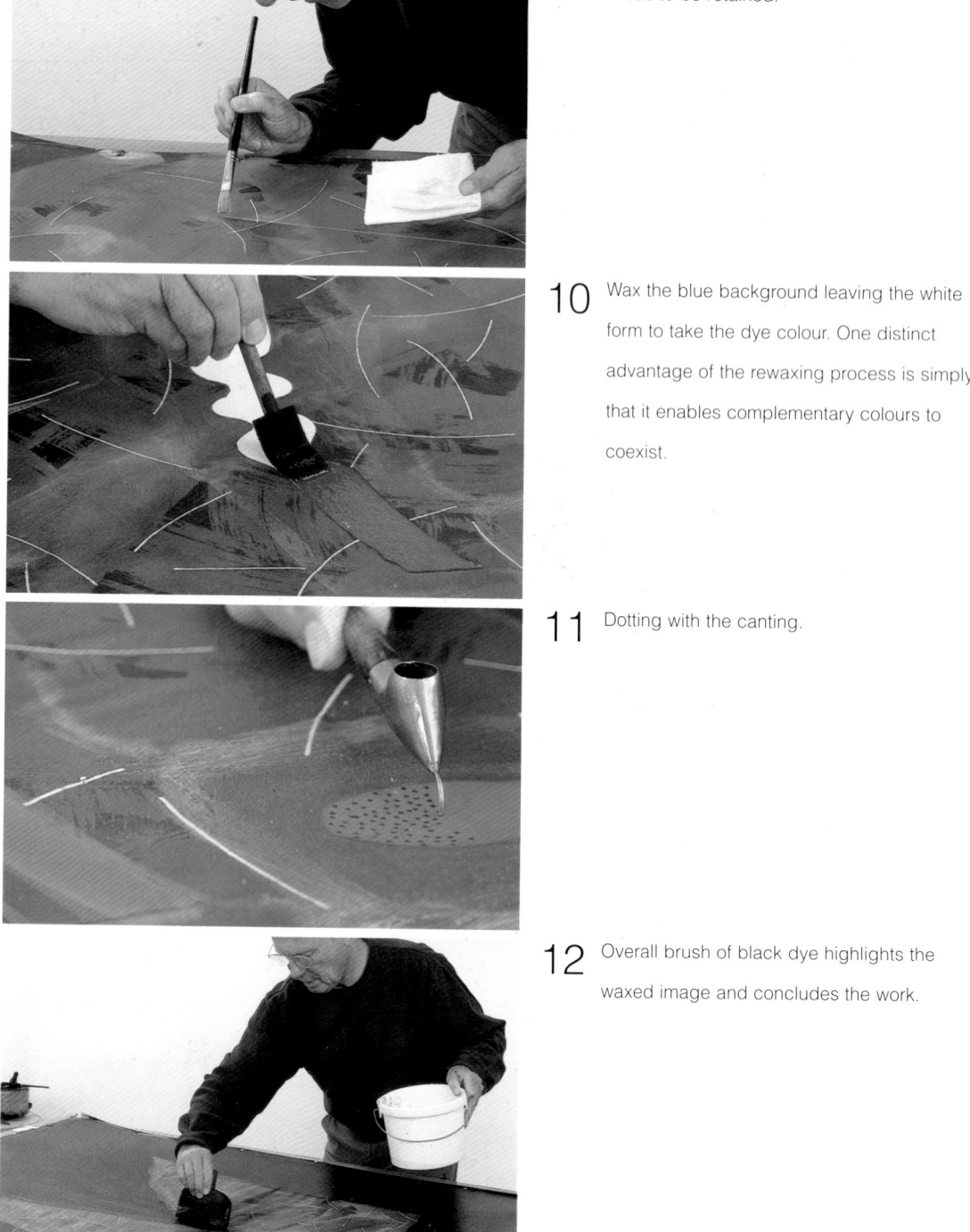

9   Place the fabric back on the frame. Rewax areas to be retained.

10   Wax the blue background leaving the white form to take the dye colour. One distinct advantage of the rewaxing process is simply that it enables complementary colours to coexist.

11   Dotting with the canting.

12   Overall brush of black dye highlights the waxed image and concludes the work.

Finished work. 13

CONCLUSION

I have attempted to demonstrate the unique and flexible nature of the wax-resist dyeing process. I trust the photographs have given a clear, practical step-by-step account of the technical options. However, it is no substitute for the experience of handling the hot wax and dye colour as it penetrates the cloth.

I recognize that the artist expects to challenge any preconceived notions. With experience, the tools and materials can be skilfully manipulated. To find self-expression, the artist is reliant on the coexistence of technique and concept. Intimate understanding and respect for the processes and materials can only reinforce the creative consciousness of the artist. Awareness and patience have their own reward.

The art of dyeing is important in this context. In the West, textile or fibre work has its emphasis on weaving; resist techniques did not exist until modern times. Japan, by contrast, has one of the most highly developed dye cultures, giving a depth of sensitivity to Japanese artists working in this medium. Appreciation of dyeing in the West can be superficial by comparison, often confusing dye work with print.

Traditional methods of dyeing can be restrictive – its practitioners coming from the point of view that the more perfected it is, the better it resists change. However, artists are prone to change and experimentation. While they respect their traditions, they will always seek to reinvent the formula on their own terms.

The cloth and the wax too have their own innate natures, and the potential they offer is fundamental to the expression of the artist's idea.

Transition Noel Dyrenforth

137 x 166 cm (54 x 65 $^1/_3$ in).

Wax-resist, reactive/discharged dyed cotton, 2001.

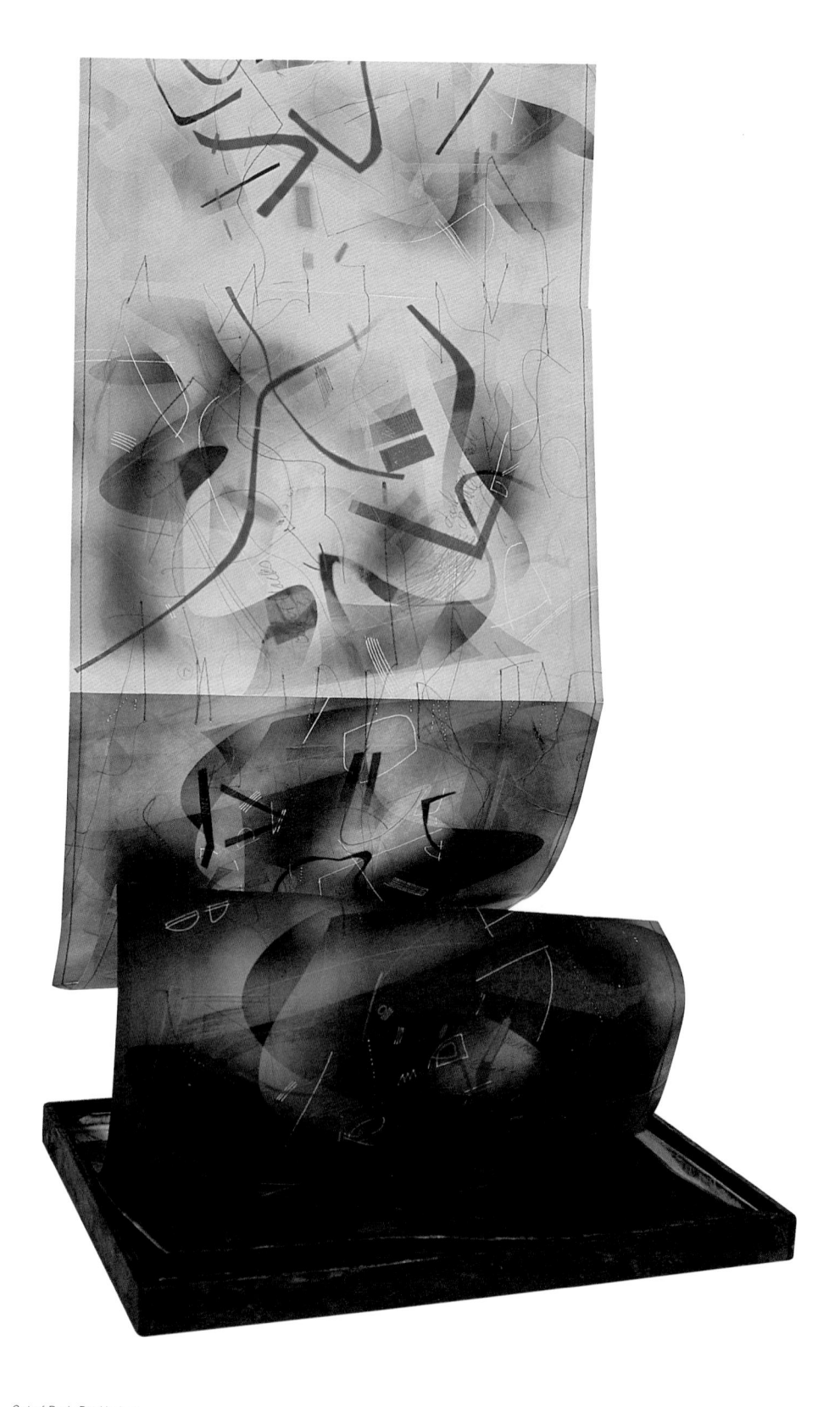

Out of Dark Pat Hodson

38 x 30 cm (15 x 12 in), unfolding to 300 cm (118 in).

Silk layered with tissue. Ink jet printed after wax-resist and

crayon-resist applied, 2000. (Photo: Michael Hodson)

Edge II Noel Dyrenforth

127 x 95 cm (50 x 37¼ in).

Wax-resist, reactive dyed/discharged on cotton, 1994. (Photo: Joël Degen)

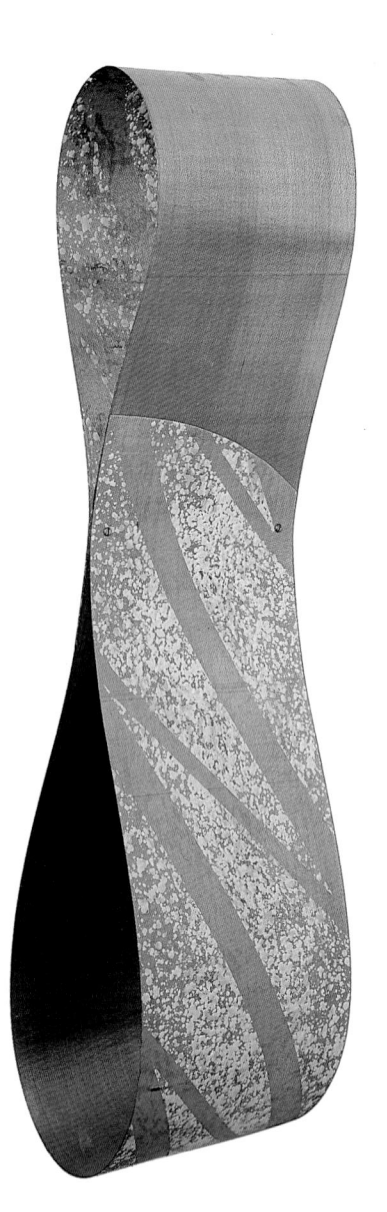

The physicality and intimacy of the medium are vital components.

Batik is a versatile process that, practised with vision, and always being ready to incorporate new properties and aesthetics, can touch the soul in this technological world. While machines have taken on many labour-intensive processes, manual skills and sensitivities such as dyeing and wax drawing can never be replaced by technology. As a consequence, batik will advance, undaunted, as a unique art medium into the 21st century.

Eight Noel Dyrenforth
90 x 50 x 30 cm
(36 x 20 x 12 in).
Wax-resist, reactive dyed on
wood veneer, 1996. (right).

Greeting cards, Noel
Dyrenforth 1990–2000 (left).

AMRI YAHIA
Born 1939 in Palembang, Sumatra, Indonesia

A leading innovative Indonesian artist who graduated from the Academy of Fine Arts, Yogyakarta in 1963 and who is a professor at the Islamic University. He founded many cultural enterprises besides his own gallery in 1972. He has travelled widely. In 1986 he was a visiting professor at Iowa State University in the USA. His work is included in many eminent collections including that of the Director General of UNESCO and the National Gallery of Kuwait. In 1998 he exhibited at the Asian Art Museum in San Francisco.

'I chose batik as a medium of art expression because of its inherent origin in the Indonesian culture, generation to generation.

'Batik is close to social daily life. It has a high and everlasting value in history and culture in our society. As a painter, I wanted to find something new; batik painting was considered a new medium and I love it and will paint with it forever. It is a supreme medium in painting. I wish to unify the earth through art!'

HETTY VAN BOEKHOUT
Born 1945 in Heerlen, the Netherlands

1967–71 Royal Academy of Fine Arts, Antwerp, Belgium
1971–73 National High Institute of Art, Antwerp
1983–2000 Lived and worked in the UK.
Teaches batik workshops in Belgium, the Netherlands and the UK.
Work in private and public collections.

'I like to emphasize the material quality and the tactile value in my work, using the specific technique of batik in an autonomous way. Collage is an important element which creates layers of 'skin'. Shapes can be moved around. The idea has a better chance of being developed without being forced.'

TONY DYER
Born 1942, Australia

1964–68 Associate Diploma of Art (RMIT)
1969–70 Fellowship Diploma of Art (RMIT)
2001 Stanthorpe Art Awards, Cancer Council 'Daffodil Art Awards', Australia
Works are included in the National Gallery of Victoria; Victoria State Craft Collection; Guizhou Provincial Museum, China; Art Gallery of Western Australia; Powerhouse Museum, Sydney; The University of Melbourne; Sale Regional Arts Gallery, Victoria; Queen Victoria Art Gallery, Launceston, Tasmania; Queensland Art Gallery; Ararat Art Gallery; Artbank; Museum and Art Gallery of the Northern Territory.

'Structure within my work is very important. It is evident within the transparent and opaque grids and stripes of the weave of the silk, where it acts as a metaphor, creating visual and structural links with the symbolism and stylized images.

'Each aspect of the total art process should be constantly reviewed, so it is most important to maintain an honest, ongoing, critical review of my work. The dynamic interaction that exists between ideas/concepts, attitude, knowledge, skills, experience, selected fabrics, waxes and dyes enables infinite possibilities to emerge.'

NOEL DYRENFORTH
Born 1936 London, UK

Studied at Central School of Art and Design (drawing and painting); Goldsmiths College, University of London (textiles); Sir John Cass School of Art (ceramic sculpture).
Worked with the batik technique since 1962. Teaches internationally.
Arts awards for exhibitions in Tokyo, Jogyakarta, Indonesia and Guizhou, China and 'Artist in Residence' Melbourne, Australia.
Over 130 mixed exhibitions, 34 solo exhibitions world-wide.

Works are included in the collections of the Victoria and Albert Museum, London; National Gallery, Melbourne, Australia; Guizhou Provincial Museum, China; Melbourne University and State College; Sembikiya Gallery, Tokyo; Galerie Smend, Cologne; Bradford City Art Gallery; Crafts Council, London; Leicester County Council Art Collection; Museum of Wales; County Education Collections, UK; private collections in the USA, Europe, Australia and Japan.

'I have never been complacent about batik. I have constantly exploited it for my own intuitive, creative ends. Method challenges concept and vice versa ... rules are broken, redefined ... risks taken! In batik the molten wax hardens in the cloth resisting the promiscuous ebb of the dye. My make-up and motivation is symbolically echoed in this reaction between definitive and organic structure.

'My recurring theme is about the cutting forces in society which intentionally confuse and fragment, divide and rule...to enslave the spirit. Submission or chaos can prevail unless the enduring self-awareness can transcend and readjust. I am an optimist... I hope my work gives a glimpse of how vigilant we have to be to protect our liberty.'

SHIGEKI FUKUMOTO
Born 1946 Kyoto, Japan

1970 MFA, Kyoto City University of Arts
1997 Professor, Osaka University of Arts
Selected exhibitions:
2000 Osaka Vision 21, Osaka (grand prize)
2001 Cheongju International Craft Biennale, Cheongju, South Korea
(invited artists prize)

Public Collections:
National Museum of Modern Art, Tokyo; National Museum of Modern Art, Kyoto; Museum of Kyoto; Osaka Foundation of Culture; Osaka 21st Century Association; Museum of Kyushu Sangyo University, Fukuoku; Cleveland Museum of Art, USA; Il-Min Museum, Seoul.

'From the creator's point of view, the special delight of Rozome can be said to lie in the way the hot wax instantly cools and hardens when it is applied to the cloth. Agile handling controls the temperature and amount of wax, allowing one to adjust the amount of wax that the cloth absorbs so that subtle differences of effect strike the eye. Through deft handling of temperature changes in the wax, the creator's feeling and emotion reveals itself in the brush flow of the moment's impulse and achieves a fixed expression directly on to the cloth. The creator must commit his or her all to the moment's victory or defeat in this instantaneous process that permits no second try. This is the hidden enchantment of Rozome that draws us into its thrall.'

PAT HODSON
Born 1944 Golborne, Lancashire, UK

Studied art at Liverpool College of Art & Design from 1963–67.

'An interest in colorants led to wide-ranging experiments in the 1970s, centred around dye colour, fibre and wax-resist. This continued to the present day with changes in approach and direction. Since 1990, the aim has been to increase emotional and visual impact of the image, using complex layering and transformation techniques.'

'All things are transitory – in a state of change. The fibre which is used for spinning into yarn or mashed into paper is itself simply arrested in a state of change that defers disintegration. In turn, the dyed image on the cloth is bleached by light – part of the natural cycle of life and rebirth.

'A single image is inadequate to explain the idea of transformation – of time-mapping the pattern of change in image or materials. A single image might have undergone many processes or ideas, each valid at the time, but inevitably hidden when the decision was taken to add another mark, motif or layer of dye. The sense of loss, of spent vitality is overwritten.

'Mapping the hidden changes which are made when an idea is explored, defines how the piece is realized as a tactile art work. It now comprises a series of images rather than one – each made from a collage of paper, silk, wax, crayon, stitch and other resists, applied to the surface before printing.

'An idea might have been entirely conceived on computer screen, on paper or from a mixture of sources: camera, watercolour or drawing.'

SHOUKOH KOBAYASHI
Born 1955 Kyoto, Japan

1978 graduated from Osaka University of Arts.
Lecturer, Faculty of Art, Kyoto University of Education.

| 1997 | Awarded Kyoto Prefectural Governor's Prize at the Kyoto Art and Craft Artists Association Exhibition. |
| 2000 | Awarded Grand Prix at the NIKKO KAI |

Collections: Kyoto Prefecture; UNESCO Paris.

'My earlier work represented the vibrant sound and vigorous power of nature. By eliminating figurative elements, only pure imagery and clear impressions filter through. However, my more recent work has changed to involve my travels and encounters with different cultures and my observations on the complicated and absurd side of modern society.'

PETER WENGER
Born 1937 Berlin, Germany

Studied batik under Richard Dölker from 1953–55. Went to the College of Art in Berlin and Cologne from 1956–62. From 1982–2001 taught batik at the Craft College in Thomastown, Ireland.

Collections: Arts Council of Ireland; private collections.

'Who can resist the spell of the luminously bright motif painted with wax, floating as it were in front of the sombre, unfathomable darkness of the dyed cloth? My main aim has always been to let this unique visual phenomenon speak for itself.'

CONVERSION TABLES OF WEIGHTS, MEASURES AND TEMPERATURE

Weight	Metric equivalent
1 ounce	28 g
4 ounces	113 g
8 ounces	227 g
16 ounces (1 pound)	454 g
2.2 pounds	1 kg

1 teaspoon approximately 3 g

Volume	Metric equivalent
$^1/_4$ teaspoon	1 ml
1 teaspoon	5 ml
1 tablespoon	15 ml
1 fluid ounce, imperial	28 ml
1 fluid ounce, US	30 ml
$^1/_2$ cup	118 ml
1 pint, imperial (20 imp. fl oz)	568 ml
1 pint, US (16 US fl oz)	473 ml
1 quart, imperial	1136 ml
1 quart, US	946 ml
1 gallon, imperial	4.55 litres
1 gallon, US	3.79 litres

All substances, dyestuffs and chemicals have different weight values and cannot be equated by volume.

Length	Metric equivalent
1 inch	2.54 cm
1 foot	0.305 m
1 yard	0.91 m
1 mile	1.61 km

Temperature conversion table
32° F = 0° C (freezing point of water)
132° F = 56° C (melting point of paraffin)
136° F = 58° C (melting point of beeswax)
166° F = 75° C (melting point of micro crystalline wax)

Acid dye These are mainly sodium salts of organic acids assisted by salt. It is an acid or acid-producing compound in the dyebath that has an affinity with silk and wool.

Affinity Special chemical attraction of a dye to the fibres of a fabric that allows them to bond together.

Aniline dyes The first synthetic dyes, made with aniline as the basis. Aniline unites with acid to form colour salts.

Assistant Chemical dye recipe that aids the bond between dye and fibre.

Azoic dyes These dyes form colour on the fibre, usually cotton, by impregnating with naphthol and then coupling with a diazo salt bath. The dyes are very fast to boiling and light and are used extensively in Javanese batiks today.

Beeswax The malleable quality of beeswax ensures a flexible and substantial resist which corrodes less than synthetic resists when chemicals (except alkali) are added.

Bleaching Process of discharging colour from fibres by chemical means.

Bleeding Loss of dye colour, usually in the washing.

Calgon Trade name of a common water-softening agent.

Canting (pronounced *chanting*, originally spelt *tjanting*). Tool for applying wax, with which hand-drawn tulis batik is made.

Cap (pronounced *chap* and originally spelt *tjap*). Copper block stamp to apply wax to cloth.

Caustic soda Sodium hydroxide is the effective agent for mercerizing cotton. It is used in naphthol and as an alkali.

Cellulose The basic material of all vegetable fibres – cotton, flax – as well as the synthetic viscose Rayon.

Chemical water (Calgon) Sodium hexametaphosphate, it acts as a sequestering agent, neutralizing any interference in water to the normal reaction of dyes.

Colour Depends on three measurable qualities: hue, degree of lightness or darkness, and intensity.

Cone drawing (tsutsugaki) Freehand style application of resist paste, using a mulberry paper brass-tipped cone.

Crocking Unfixed dye which rubs off cloth surface.

Dip Immersion of cloth into dye bath.

Direct application Includes painting on, spraying, and blocking the dyes, pigments or resists on to the surface of the cloth.

Direct dyes A cotton dye, simple to apply with the addition of salt. Fastness is poor, but can be improved with after-treatment.

Discharge Removal of colour, also called bleaching or stripping.

Dodot Batik cloth made by joining two kains together (2 x 4 m, 6.5 x 13 ft) used for ceremonial occasions.

Dressing A mixture applied to manufactured fabric to give a finish to the cloth surface. Best removed before dyeing.

Dry cleaning Cleaning fabric by treating with an organic solvent.

Dye bath Solution of dyestuff, assistants and water in which the cloth is immersed.

Exhaust The degree by which the cloth takes up the full colour potential of the dye bath.

Fastness The cloth's colour resistance, particularly to light and washing.

Fibre-reactive dyes MX cold-water dye which reacts to alkaline solution to form a bond between the dye molecule and the fibre. It is inter-mixable (to vary colour), reliable, fast and simple to use on cotton and silk.

Fixing The process of making the colour permanent to ensure fastness.

Garuda Mythical bird of Indonesia, symbol of heaven.

Glauber's salt Sodium sulphate which encourages level dyeing.

Gringsing A fish-scale motif which patterns the background of Indonesian batiks.

Gutta Gutta-percha is a colourless rubber latex used as a resist. It is applied to the material with either a plastic pipette or cone.

Hera Spatula used for applying resist paste through a stencil.

Hikizome brush A ground-colour brush with wide handle and deer-hair bristles. It absorbs large amounts of dye.

Ikat Wrapping yarns to a pattern resist, dyed and woven.

Ikat kapala Batik head cloth.

Indigo Made from the leaves of the plant *Indigofera*, this dye is distributed widely throughout the tropical areas of the world. Historically indigo is the oldest and most important of dyestuffs. Synthetic indigo came on to the market in 1897 and was soon cheaper and more convenient to use than the natural product.

Kain panjang Long cloth, approximately 2–3 metres (6.5–10 ft) long, densely decorated with batik designs and with border at one end.

Katazome Paste-resist stencil dyeing.

Kemben A narrow batik cloth used around the upper body to fasten a sarong.

Kepala The perpendicular band that contrasts with the main design area of the sarong.

Kraton Javanese palace.

Kyokechi Japanese term for a clamp resist, particularly used during the Nara period. Fabric was clamped between perforated wooden boards and dyed.

Ladao A wax tool used by the minority peoples of Central Asia.

Levelling agent An assistant that promotes the level distribution of colour on the cloth.

Liquid ratio The ratio (measured by weight) of the water in a dye bath to the weight of the cloth.

Lissapol Detergent and wetting agent.

Ludigol Chemical that prevents reduction.

Lye Caustic soda (sodium hydroxide) solution.

Mercerizing Treatment of cellulose cloth with concentrated caustic soda to improve lustre and strengthen the fibres' affinity with the dye.

Micro crystalline wax Synthetic substance derived from petroleum. It is used as a substitute for beeswax.

Migration Movement of dye from one part of the cloth to another.

Monopol brilliant oil Stabilizer and softener for naphthol dye bath.

Mordant Chemical that combines with the dye molecule in the cloth to form an insoluble compound.

Naphthol dyes See Azoic dyes.

Nori Rice-paste resist.

Overdyeing Placing one colour dye over another.

Oxidation Exposure of the dyed cloth to oxygen in the air; in vat dyeing this converts the colour back into its insoluble form to bond it to the fibre.

Pagi-sore A batik sarong which can be adjusted to be worn as morning or evening wear. Each half has a separate design.

Paraffin wax Soft, translucent wax derived from petroleum. It is brittle and less resistant than micro crystalline wax. Marbling effects are created by using a greater percentage of paraffin in the recipe.

Parang A diagonal 'broken knife' batik motif on a sarong, at one time worn exclusively by the nobility in Java.

Pigment Powder forms mixed with a resin-bound are coated onto the fabric, giving an opacity and slight stiffening to the texture.

Plangi Technique of resist tying and dyeing cloth.

Prepared for printing Fabric that has been scoured, degummed and bleached.

Protein fibre Animal material for making wool and silk.

Rayon Artificial fibre made from cellulose. Viscose Rayon dyes as well as cotton.

Resist salt L A mild oxidizing agent that prevents the dye from decomposing during fixation and achieves a high colour yield.

Roketsu-zome Japanese batik method of wax-resist dyeing.

Salt Sodium chloride used as an assistant in reactive and direct dyes.

Sarong Javanese or Malay waist cloth, originally from India.

Scouring Removing impurities from fabric by washing in soap or detergent in preparation for dyeing.

Shading Adding a small quantity of dye to increase colour shade.

Shibori Tie-dye patterns that are reserved by pressing, stitching or binding before immersion in a dye bath.

Shrinkage Contraction of cloth from heat or moisture processes.

Sizing Application of starch or coating agent to enhance finish on cloth.

Slendang Long, narrow cloth used by Javanese women.

Soda ash Mild alkali, known as sodium carbonate (a form of washing soda) causes Procion M dyes to react in fibre.

Sodium alginate (Manutex) A gum extract from seaweed used as a thickening agent.

Sodium bicarbonate (baking powder) A mild alkaline used in reactive dyeing for painting on colour.

Sodium bisulphite A quick, inexpensive chemical for discharge dyeing. It contains chlorine.

Sodium hydrosulphite A less powerful discharge agent than chlorine bleach.

Soga Rich brown dye derived mainly from tree bark.

Steaming Moist heat process for fixing dye colour.

Stock solution Prepared chemical or dye solution to a specific ratio.

Synthetic dyes The early man-made dyes made from the aniline contained in coal tar were not particularly successful. It was not until 1868 with the discovery of synthetic alizarin that they replaced the natural product commercially.

Thickener A gel-like substance used to increase the consistency in painting on dye.

Tsutsugaki Refer to cone drawing.

Tulis The hand-drawn batik method.

Tumpal A band designed with triangles that run down the ends of a batik sarong.

Union dye A dye mixture suited to two or more blended fibres.

Urea A mild alkali synthesized from natural gas, used as a moisture-retaining agent.

Vat dyes These dyes are insoluble in water and must be dissolved chemically before being applied to fabric. Colour develops by exposure to heat and light or an oxidizing agent. Suitable for cotton and silk.

Vinegar Contains acetic acid and is used in dyeing silk and wool; to prevent staining, do not use a dark vinegar.

Washing off To wash surplus dye or ingredients out of cloth, to prevent them interfering with further dyeing of the cloth or the natural finished texture.

Whetting out To assure more even and level colour, the cloth is dampened before dyeing.

Yuzen A particular fine dye painting style contained by resist-paste outlines.

BIBLIOGRAPHY

Benjamin, Betsy Sterling, *The World of Rozome, Wax-Resist Textiles of Japan*, Tokyo: Kodansha International, 1996

Bois, Mechteld de, *Chris Lebeau 1878–1945*, Assen and Haarlem: Drent Museum/Frans Hals Museum, 1985

Broughton, Kate, *Textile Dyeing*, Rockport, Massachusetts: Rockport Publishers, 1995

Djoenena, Nian, *Batik – Its Mystery and Meaning*, Jakarta: Djambaran, 1986

Dyrenforth, Noel (with John Houston), *Batik with Noel Dyrenforth*, London: Orbis, 1975; Dutch version: Amsterdam: Uitgeverij Kosmos, 1977

Dyrenforth, Noel, *The Technique of Batik*, B T Batsford, 1988; Reprinted (paperback), 1997

Elliott, Inger McCabe, *Batik – Fabled Cloth of Java*, New York: Clarkson N. Potter Inc., 1984

Flower, Lynda, *Ideas and Techniques for Fabric Design*, London: Longman, 1986

Foreman, B., *Indonesian Batik and Ikat*, London: Hamlyn, 1988

Fukumoto, Shigeki, 'Japan and the Art of Dyeing', *Japan ECO Times*, May/June/July 1993

Gittinger, Mattiebelle, *Splendid Symbols, Textiles and Traditions in Indonesia*, New Haven, Connecticut: Eastern Press, 1979

Gittinger, Mattiebelle, *Indonesian Textiles*, Washington, DC: Textile Museum, 1980

Gittinger, Mattiebelle, *To Speak with Cloth, Studies in Indonesian Textiles*, Museum of Cultural History, 1989

Haake, Annegret, *Javanische Batik, Methode–Symbolik–Geschichte*, Hannover: M & H Schaper, 1984

Harrod, Tanya, *The Crafts in Britain in the Twentieth Century*, Tate University Press, 1999

Holt, Claire, *Art in Indonesia: Continuity & Change*, Ithaca, New York: Cornell University Press, 1967

Hout, Itie van, *Batik Drawn in Wax*, Amsterdam: Royal Tropical Institute/KIT Publishers, 2001

Hunter, I., *Dyeing with Fibre-Reactive Dyes*, Sydney: Batik Oetoro, 1977

Hunter, I., *Dyeing with Naphthol Dyes*, Sydney: Batik Oetoro, 1977

ICI Dyestuffs Division, *Introduction to Textile Printing*, London: Butterworth, 1964

Larsen, Jack Lenor, *The Dyer's Art*, New York: Van Norstrand Reinhold, 1976

Loeber, J A, *Das Batiken in Blüte, Indonesisches Künstlerleben*, Gerhard Stelling, 1925

Maxwell, John and Robyn, *Textiles of Indonesia*, Melbourne: Gardner, 1976

Mijer, P., *Batiks and How to Make Them*, New York: Dodd Mead, 1925

Meilach, Dona, *Contemporary Batik and the Dye*, London: Allen & Unwin, 1973

Monzie, A. de, *Les Batiks de Madame Pangon*, Paris: Charles Moreau, 1925

Moyer, Susan Louise, *Silk Painting, The Artists Guide To Gutta and Wax Techniques*, New York: Watson-Guptill, 1991

Nakano, Eisha (with B Stephan), *Japanese Stencil Dyeing*, New York and Tokyo: Weatherhill, 1982

Nea, Sara, *Batik*, New York: Van Norstrand Reinhold, 1970

Picton, John and MACK, J, *African Textiles*, London: British Museum, 1979

Piper, Eloise, *Batik for Artists and Quilters*, Search Press, 2001

Proctor, Richard and LEW, Jennifer, *Surface Design for Fabric*, Seattle: University of Washington Press, 1984

Raffles, Thomas Stamford, *The History of Java* (reprint of 1817 Edition), Kuala Lumpur: Oxford University Press, 1982

Robinson, Rosi, *Creative Batik*, Search Press, 2001

ROBINSON, Stuart, *The History of Dyed Textiles*, London: Studio Vista, 1969

Smend, Rudolf, *Seidenmalerei Handbuch V*, Cologne: Galerie Smend, 1993

Smend, Rudolf, *25 Jahre Textile Kunst*, Cologne: Galerie Smend, 1998

Smend, Rudolf, *Javanese & Sumatran Batiks*, Cologne: Galerie Smend, 2000

Soeiopo, S., *Batik*, Jakarta: P.E. Indira, 1983

Spee, Miep, *Traditional & Modern Batiks*, Kangaroo Press, 1977

Steinmann, Alfred, 'Batiks', *CIBA Review*, 58 (1947.

Steinmann, Alfred, *Batik – A Survey of Batik Design*, F. Lewis, 1958

Storey, Joyce, *Dyes and Fabrics*, London and New York: Thames & Hudson, 1978

Sutton, Anne, *British Craft Textiles*, London: William Collins, 1985

Thomas, Michael, *Textile Art*, London: Weidenfeld & Nicolson, 1985

Ursin, A. and Kilchenmann, *Batik – Harmonie mit Wachs und Farbe*, Berne: Paul Haupt, 1979

Veldhuisen, Harmen C., *Batik Belinda 1840–1940: Dutch Influence in Batik from Java*, Jakarta: Dr. Gaya Favorit Press, 1993

Victoria & Albert Museum, *Batiks*, London: HMSO, 1969

Victoria & Albert Museum, *The Victoria & Albert Museum's Textile Collection from 1940 to the Present*, London: V&A, 1999

Warming, Wanda and Gaworski, Michael, *The World of Indonesian Textiles*, Tokyo: Kodansha International, 1981

Wells, Kate, *Fabric Dyeing and Printing*, London: Conran Octopus, 1997

Australia

Suppliers

Batik Oetoro
203 Avoca Street
Randwick
NSW 2031
Tel: 612 9398 6201
Fax: 612 9398 1173
www.dyeman.com
(Fibre-reactives, naphthol,
indigosol, vat dyes,acid
dyes, chemicals, waxes,
silk, cotton, imports
of Javanese cotton,
cantings and stoves.
Excellent information
sheets on dyeing and
waxing recipes. Mail order.)

Kraftkolour
242 High Street
Northcote
Victoria 3070
Tel: 613 9482 9234
Fax: 613 9482 9279
kkolour@vegas.com.au

Periodicals

Craft Arts International
PO Box 363
Neutral Bay Junction 2089
Sydney, NSW
Tel: 612 9908 4797
Fax: 612 9953 1576
info@craftart.com.au

Craft Australia
Level 5
414–18 Elizabeth Street
Surrey Hills
NSW 2010
Tel: 612 9211 1445
Fax: 612 9211 1443
craft@craftaustralia.com.au

Object
Centre for Contemporary
Craft and Design

3rd Floor, Customs House
31 Alfred Street
Circular Quay
Sydney
NSW 2000
Tel: 612 9247 9126
Fax: 612 9247 2641
object@object.com.au

Organizations

Australian Batik & Surface
Design Association Inc.
PO Box 43
Gladesville
NSW 2111

Crafts Council of Australia
100 George Street
The Rocks
Sydney
NSW 2000
(Represents craftspeople,
arranges exhibitions
and produces slides,
books and periodicals.)

TAFTA
The Australian Forum for
Textile Arts Ltd
PO Box 38
The Gap 4061
Queensland
Tel: 617 3300 6491
Fax: 617 3300 2148
tafta@uq.net.au

Museums

National Museum of
Victoria
180 St Kilda Road
Melbourne
Victoria 3004

Belgium

Suppliers

Ballannekee
Patriottenstraat 35
B2600 Berchem
Antwerp
Tel: 32 3 2308375

(Batik supplies and
workshops.)

Textile Centrum Rita
Trefois
Lijnmolenstraat 52
B9042 Ghent
Tel: 32 9 2291849
Fax: 32 9 2291528
(Workshops)

La Fourmi
Vanderkindere 211
B1180 Brussels
Tel: 32 2 3458465
Fax: 32 2 3437141
(Dyes, fabric, batik
equipment. Mail order.)

Canada

Suppliers

Maiwa Handprints
1606 Johnston Street
Vancouver
British Columbia
V6H 3S2
Tel: 604 669 3939
Fax: 604 669 0609

China

Museums

Guizhou Batik Art
Academy
270 Waihuan Dong Road
Guiyang
Guizhou

France

Suppliers

H. Dupont
86 Rue de Clery
F75002 Paris
(Manufacturer of batik,
silk/wool painting
dyes and gutta)

Kniazeff
Atelier Creatiff
18 Rue de Garet
F69001 Lyons
(Silk/wool painting dyes)

Sennelier

Rue de Moulin a Cailloux
Orley, Senia
408-9456-1 Rungis Cedex
(Manufacturer of Tinfix
silk/wool dyes)

Germany

Suppliers

Deka-Textilfarben GmbH
Kapellenstrasse 18
D82008 Unterhaching
Tel: 089 6650640
(Manufacturer of Deka L
and Deka silk dyes)

Galerie Smend
Mainzer Strasse 31, 37
Postfach 250450
D50678 Cologne
Tel: 0221 312047
Fax: 0221 9320718
smend@smend.de
www.smend.de
(batik materials:
Re-active dyes,
Princecolour, silk
dyes, gutta, waxes,
Javanese cantings,
fabrics,books and
periodicals. Comprehensive
mail order catalogue and
service. Textile art
workshop programme.)

Höchst AG
Brüningstrasse 50
D65929 Frankfurt
Tel: 069 3050
(Manufacturer of anthrasol,
naphthol-AS,
ramazol)

Periodicals

Kunst und Handwerk
Duisburger Strasse 82
D40479 Düsseldorf
Tel: 0211 4911331

Textilforum (German and
English editions)
Friedenstrasse 5
Postfach 5944
D30175 Hannover
Tel: 0511 817007
Fax: 0511 813108

tfs@ETN-net.org
http:/www.ETN-net.org/tfs

Textilkunst
Verlag M & H Schaper
Postfach 1642
D31061 Alfeld-am-Leine
Tel: 0581 800914
Fax: 0581 800933
info@schaper-verlag.de

Museums
Deutsches Textilmuseum
Andreasmarkt 8
D47809 Krefeld
Tel: 02151 9469450

Gallerie Smend
see under 'suppliers'
*(Contemporary and
traditional batik
collection, study and
library area.)*

Netherlands

Suppliers
Zijdelings
Karina van Vught
Kepelstraat 93a
5048CL Tilburg
*(Procion, ramazol, batik
equipment, fabric.)*

Periodicals
Textiel Plus
Wilhelminaweg 12
34441 XC Woerden
Tel: 0348 460958
Fax: 0348 460802
textiel.plus@worldonline.nl

Museums
Royal Tropical Institute
P O Box 95001
Mauritskade 63
Amsterdam
Tel: 31 20 5688200

Stedelijk Museum
Paulus Potterstraat 13
Amsterdam
Tel: 31 20 5732911
Nederlands Textile
Museum
Goirkestraat 96
5046 GN Tilburg
Tel: 0135 422241

India
Organizations
Batik Art Research and
Training Institute
50 Silwat Wari
Udaipur
Rajasthan

Indonesia

Suppliers
Sawojajar
Jl Panerbahan 1
Yogyakarta
Java
*(Cantings, resin, wax;
primissima, prima,
biro and merah qualities of
cotton; Naphthol
and indigosol dyes.)*

Organizations
Batik Research Centre
Jl Kusumanegara 2
Yogyakrta
Java

Galleries
Amri Yahya Gallery
Jl Gampingan 62
Yogyakarta 55253
Java
Tel: 62 274 564525
Fax: 62 274 588980
galeriamri@eudoramail.com

Kuswadji Gallery
Jl Alun Alun Utara Pojok
Barat Daya
Yogyakarta
Java

Tulus Warsito Gallery
JL Jogokanyan 69B
Mantrijeron
Yogyakarta, Java

Japan

Suppliers
Seiwa Inc.
1-1-1 Shimo-achiai
Shinjuku-ku
Tokyo 169
Tel: 03 3364 2112
Fax: 03 3304 2115
*(Dyes, wax, brushes,
steamers, fabric.
Mail order.)*

Tanaka Nao Dyes Supplies
Sanjodori Ogawa Nishi-iru
Nakagyo-ku
Kyoto 690
Tel: 075 221 4112
Fax: 075 221 0276
and
Takara Building 3F
1-26-30 Higashi
Shibuya-ku
Tokyo 150
*Tel: 03 3400 4844
Fax: 03 3400 4969
(Dyes, chemicals, fabric,
wax, roketsu-zome and
katazome supplies. Mail
order.)*

Organizations
Japan Craft Design
Association
21-23 Sendagaya-1
Shibuya-ku
Tokyo 151

Kyoto International
Contemporary Textile Art
Centre
Kotobuki Building 5F
Kawaramachi
Shijo-sagarui
Shimogyo-ku
Kyoto 600
Tel/Fax: 075 341 1501
*(International exchange
and promotion of
textile art.)*

Periodicals
Textile Arts Magazine
Shikosha Publishing Co.
Ltd
Kyoto

Senshoku
Senshoku To Seikatsu-sha
Publishers
Matsubara-dori
Karasuma Nishi-iru
Shimagyo-ku
Kyoto 600
Tel: 075 343 0388
Fax: 075 343 0399

Switzerland

Museums
Museum fur Völkerkunde,
Basel

United Kingdom

Suppliers
Candle Makers Suppliers
28 Blythe Road
London W14 0HA
Tel: 020 7602 4031
Fax: 020 7602 2796
candles@candlemakers.co
.uk
*(Procion, Kniazeff, Deka
dyes, beeswax and
synthetic waxes, cantings,
videos, books and helpful
advice. Mail order.)*

Kemtex Colours
Chorley Business and
Technology Centre
Euxton Lane
Chorley PR7 6TE
Tel: 01257 230220
Fax: 01257 230225
www.kemtex.co.uk

Macculloch & Wallis Ltd
25 Dering Street
London W15 1AT
Tel: 020 7629 0311
Fax: 020 7491 2481
(cottons and silks)

Pongees Ltd
28 Hoxton Square
London N1
Tel: 020 7739 9130
Fax: 020 7739 9132
*(silks, crepe satin, crepe
de chine, habotai, spun,
twill.)*

Poth Hille & Co Ltd
37 High Street
Stratford
London E15 2QD
Tel: 020 8534 7091
*(waxes, including micro,
paraffin and
beeswax.)*

Textile Techniques
37 High Street
Bishop's Castle
Shropshire SY9 5BE
Tel/Fax: 01588 638712
*(Javanese cantings and
fabric, wax and dye.)*

George Weil & Fibrecrafts
Old Portsmouth Road

Peasmarsh
Guildford
Surrey GU7 2NG
Tel: 01483 565800
Fax: 01483 565807
sales@georgeweil.co.uk
www.georgeweil.co.uk
*(Comprehensive fibre art
suppliers. Procion, acid,
indigo dyes, batik
equipment and materials.
Book list and
mail order catalogue.)*

Whaleys (Bradford) Ltd
Harris Court
Great Horton
Bradford BD7 4EQ
Tel: 01274 576718
Fax: 01274 521309
*(Silk, cotton, calico, jute,
linen and wool.)*

Organizations
Contemporary Applied
Arts
2 Percy Street
London W1P 9FA
Tel: 020 7436 2344
www.caa.org.uk

Crafts Council
44a Pentonville Road
London N1 9BY
Tel: 020 7278 7700
craftscouncil.org.uk

The Batik Guild
Membership: 16 St. Paul's
Place
London N1 2QE
Tel: 020 7226 3744

Periodicals
Crafts
44a Pentonville Road
London N1 9BY
Tel: 020 7806 2538

Fax: 020 7837 0858
crafts@craftscouncil.org.uk

*Hali: The International
Magazine for Carpet and
Textile Art*
Hali Publications Limited
St Giles House
50 Poland Street
London W1V 4AX
Fax: 020 7940 4897
hali@centaur.co.uk

Museums and Galleries
The British Museum
Great Russell Street
London WC1
Tel: 020 7323 8000
information@thebritishmus
eum.ac.uk

Joss Graham Textile
Gallery
10 Eccleston Street
London SW1 0LT
Tel/Fax: 020 7730 4370

Victoria & Albert Museum
South Kensington
London SW7 2RL
Tel: 020 7942 2000
vanda@vam.ac.uk

United States

Suppliers
Aljo Manufacting Co. Ltd
81 Franklin Street
New York
NY 10013
Tel: 212 966 4046
Fax: 212 274 9616
*(Chemicals and dyes:
acid, basic, direct,
reactive, naphthol and
vat.)*

Dharma Trading Company

PO Box 150916
San Rafael
CA 94915
Te.: 415 456 7657
Fax: 415 456 8747
*(Comprehensive range of
textile dyes and
equipment.)*

Pro-Chemical & Dye Inc
PO Box 14
Somerset
Massachusetts 02726
Tel: 508 676 3838
Fax: 508 676 3980

Wild Fibre
Art Studio and Store
1453E 14th Street
Santa Monica
CA 90404
Tel: 800 382 7067

Organizations
AmericanCrafts Council
72 Spring Street
New York
NY 10012

Surface Design
Association
PO Box 360
Sebastopol
CA 95473
www.surfacedesign.org

Periodicals
American Crafts
72 Spring Street
New York
NY 10012-4019

Fibrearts
Lark Communication
50 College Street
Asheville
North Carolina 28801
Tel: 828 253 0467

Fax: 828 253 7952
fibrearts@larkbooks.com

Surface Design Journal
Surface Design
Association
see 'organizations'

Museums and Galleries
American Craft Museum
40 West 53rd Street
New York
NY 10019

Textile Museum
2320 S. Street NW
Washington, DC

Textile Study Centre
University of Washington
Seattle